D1560247

Chachie Dupuy's
NEW ORLEANS
HOME COOKING

Chachie Dupuy's
NEW ORLEANS
HOME COOKING

A Bobbs-Merrill Book

Macmillan Publishing Company
New York

Collier Macmillan Publishers
London

We gratefully acknowledge the following sources for the photographs included in this volume.

The Library of Congress: Frontispiece and pages vi, 32, 40, 62, 72 (photograph by Carl Mydans), and 126 (photograph by John Teunisson).

The National Archives: pages 80 and 166.

Macmillan Publishing Company
866 Third Avenue, New York, N.Y. 10022
Collier Macmillan Canada, Inc.

Library of Congress Cataloging-in-Publication Data
Dupuy, Chachie.
    Chachie Dupuy's New Orleans home cooking.
    Rev. ed. of: Chachie's New Orleans cooking. c1984.
    "A Bobbs-Merrill book."
    Includes index.
    1. Cookery, American—Louisiana style.   2. Cookery—Louisiana—
New Orleans.   3. New Orleans (La.)—Social life and customs.
I. Dupuy, Chachie. New
Orleans cooking.   II. Title.   III. Title: New Orleans home cooking.
TX715.D893   1985b   641.59763'35   85-15468
ISBN 0-02-534290-8

Macmillan books are available at special discounts for bulk purchases for sales promotions, premiums, fund-raising, or educational use. For details, contact:

    Special Sales Director
    Macmillan Publishing Company
    866 Third Avenue
    New York, N.Y. 10022

10 9 8 7 6 5 4 3 2 1

Printed in the United States of America

Contents

Preface   vii
    Appetizers & First Courses   1
    Soups & Stews   21
    Eggs, Cheese & Luncheon Dishes   33
    Meats   41
    Poultry   53
    Fish & Shellfish   63
    Pasta, Rice & Grits   73
    Vegetables   81
    Salads   99
    Sauces & Accompaniments   107
    Breads   117
    Desserts   127
New Orleans Dinner Menus   161
Glossary   167
Mail-Order Information for
    Louisiana Products   171
Acknowledgments   173
Index   175

Preface

I remember walks through my old New Orleans neighborhood just around suppertime. Passing beneath the moss-laden oak trees, I savored the enticing aromas flowing through the open kitchen windows. It was easy to envision what each family was having for dinner.

Cooks spent their afternoons preparing those delectable daily feasts. They took great pride in cooking from scratch. Without cookbooks, their secrets were locked in a dash of this or a soupçon of that, what we know as "to taste." In a city where food is a great passion, obsession, and fascination, much of the best cooking is still done in the home. A visitor soon learns why.

Few native New Orleanians move away. They are deeply rooted in the slow, pleasure-loving, carefree tropical life of a city more than two hundred and sixty-five years old. Natives who do leave are soon lured back by the magnetic attraction of the city. The fact that families have lived in this same city for six or seven generations is the key to the high and consistent quality of food in New Orleans. Native palates are formed from childhood.

I often sat in the kitchen and watched the family cook Williana Pinkins as she worked. Williana came from Donaldsonville, Louisiana, just up the Mississippi River from New Orleans. She has been with the Dupuy family for more than thirty years. Williana never measures ingredients. I once asked her how she learned to be such a good cook. She replied, "I don't know how old I was when I started watching my mother cook, maybe ten or twelve years old. But that's how I learned. In my teens, I used to cook just about all of the recipes I still cook today. We used cast-iron pots and cooked mostly vegetables, soup, and gumbo. In those days, we didn't have all the fancy dishes we have today. We never had a cookbook at home. We just threw things together. I cook from scratch; I don't even measure seasonings."

Williana's recipes and others that have been passed down through generations are captured in this book. The recipes are written with precise measurements, easy-to-follow directions, and modern ingredients so that all cooks may enjoy these savory Creole tastes.

The exotic flavor of New Orleans food is greatly influenced by the abundant resources of the Mississippi Delta and the Gulf of Mexico. The tastes are a Creole blend of French, Spanish, African, and West Indian—a gastronomic carnival of Grillades and Grits, Red Beans and Rice, Gumbo, Jambalaya, and Étouffée.

I am often asked, "What do people who *live* in New Orleans eat? Certainly they can't eat the rich restaurant food *all* the time." This book answers that question and offers an experience in the home-style eating habits of New Orleans families. It preserves those traditional tastes—simple and sophisticated—for which the city is famous.

With a strong Creole love of good food and an endless pursuit of new tastes, I dedicate this book to those people with similar pursuits, and to the many people who contributed their support. I also dedicate this book to my parents, Charlotte and Homer, who endowed me with such epicurean passion, to Williana who taught me from childhood how to cook, and, most of all, to my husband Randy, who survived the endless hours of cooking, testing, and editing.

—Chachie Dupuy

1985

Chachie Dupuy's
NEW ORLEANS
HOME COOKING

APPETIZERS & FIRST COURSES

New Orleans is a party city. Its people enjoy good food and good company, during the week as well as on weekends. They celebrate life with such festivals as the Sugar Bowl, Mardi Gras, Spring Fiesta, Jazz and Heritage Festival, St. Joseph's Day, St. Patrick's Day, and Bastille Day. They also enjoy parties at clubs and at home. Food is often the center of attraction at these festivities.

When friends "pass by the house" (as they say in New Orleans), a late afternoon visit soon turns into a pleasant few hours of conversation. Drinks and appetizers are served on the porch. Life slows down and the "easy livin' " style is maintained.

Avocado Dip

1   ripe avocado, peeled and seeded
1   medium-sized onion, minced
1   cup Mayonnaise (page 111)
¼   teaspoon dried thyme
¼   teaspoon dried basil
¼   teaspoon dried rosemary
¼   teaspoon dried sage
¼   teaspoon dried marjoram
1   cup sour cream
1   pound crackers or potato chips

Put the avocado into a mixing bowl and mash it into a smooth paste. Add the remaining ingredients, except the crackers or potato chips, and mix very well. Cover the bowl tightly and refrigerate until serving time. Serve with the crackers or potato chips.

Yield: 2 cups; 10 servings.

Red Bean Dip

1½   cups drained cooked red kidney beans (page 88), or
      substitute drained canned red kidney beans
1   teaspoon ground black pepper
½   teaspoon salt
⅛   teaspoon Tabasco sauce, or to taste
1   pound potato chips or crackers

Put all the ingredients, except the potato chips or crackers, into the container of a blender. Blend until they are puréed. Add more seasonings, if desired. Serve with the potato chips or crackers.

Yield: 1½ cups; 8 servings.

Dill Dip

This is a light dip. For a thicker consistency, use less onion.

1   large cucumber, trimmed, washed, seeded, and cut into large chunks
1   small onion, quartered and the layers separated
½   cup apple cider vinegar
½   cup water
¼   cup sugar
8   ounces cream cheese at room temperature
2   tablespoons plain yogurt
¼   teaspoon salt
¼   teaspoon ground black pepper
3   tablespoons ground dill
1   pound potato chips or crackers or an equivalent amount of raw vegetables, such as carrot sticks, celery sticks, sweet green pepper strips, and cauliflower and broccoli flowerets

In a medium-sized bowl, mix together the cucumber, onion, vinegar, water, and sugar. Cover the bowl tightly and refrigerate overnight.

About an hour before serving, drain the liquid from the bowl. Mince the cucumber and onion pieces and drain again.

Put the chopped mixture into the container of a blender. Add the cream cheese, yogurt, salt, pepper, and dill. Blend on low speed for 1 or 2 minutes, or until the mixture is smooth. Transfer to a serving bowl, cover, and chill for 1 hour. Serve with the potato chips, crackers, or raw vegetables.

Yield: 2 cups; 6 servings.

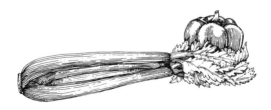

Chipped Beef Dip

8 ounces cream cheese at room temperature
2 tablespoons milk
1 2½-ounce jar chipped beef, finely chopped
2 tablespoons minced onion
1 tablespoon minced sweet green pepper
⅛ teaspoon ground black pepper
½ cup sour cream
¼ cup finely chopped pecans
1 pound corn chips or crackers

Preheat the oven to 350 degrees.

In a large bowl, blend the cream cheese and milk together. Stir in the chipped beef, onion, green pepper, black pepper, and sour cream. Mix well. Transfer the mixture to a small baking dish and sprinkle the pecans over the top. Bake, uncovered, for 20 minutes. Serve hot with the corn chips or crackers.

Yield: 8 servings.

Trout Mousse Dip

This dip can be kept hot in a chafing dish or Brûlot Bowl over a low flame.

1 pound trout fillets
1 cup Béchamel Sauce (page 110)
¼ teaspoon salt
¼ teaspoon ground black pepper
1 tablespoon fresh lemon juice
1 egg, beaten
2 egg yolks, beaten
½ cup heavy cream
1 teaspoon butter or margarine
1 pound whole wheat crackers

Preheat the oven to 350 degrees.

Use a sharp knife to chop the trout into a paste. Put the chopped trout into a large mixing bowl and add all the remaining ingredients, except the butter and crackers. Mix well.

Spread the butter over the bottom and sides of a 1-quart baking dish. Pour the trout mixture into the baking dish. Place the dish in a large roasting pan. Pour in enough hot water to come halfway up the sides of the baking dish. Bake for 1 to 1½ hours. If necessary, add more water to the roasting pan. The mousse is done when a knife inserted in the center comes out clean. Serve warm with the crackers.

Yield: 6 servings.

Oyster and Mushroom Dip

¼	cup unbleached white flour
¼	cup vegetable oil
4	shallots, minced
2	celery stalks, minced
1½	pounds fresh mushrooms, cleaned and minced
24	fresh oysters, shucked
½	cup oyster liquor
1	garlic clove, minced
1	teaspoon chopped fresh parsley leaves
½	teaspoon salt
½	teaspoon ground black pepper
1	pound corn chips or crackers

In a large heavy skillet, heat the flour and oil over medium heat. Mix thoroughly, stirring constantly with a wooden spoon until the mixture begins to bubble. Cook the roux, stirring constantly, until it turns a light brown.

Add the shallots and celery and cook over medium heat for about 10 minutes, or until the celery is soft.

Add the mushrooms, oysters, oyster liquor, and garlic. Cook, uncovered, over low heat until the mushrooms are tender and the sauce thickens, about 15 to 20 minutes. Add the parsley, salt, and pepper and stir well. Serve hot with the corn chips or crackers.

Yield: 3 cups; 8 servings.

Olive-Cheese Balls

4	ounces sharp Cheddar cheese, grated
4	tablespoons butter or margarine at room temperature
¼	teaspoon Tabasco sauce
1	teaspoon Worcestershire sauce
¾	cup unbleached white flour
1	3-ounce jar pimiento-stuffed olives, drained

Preheat the oven to 400 degrees.

In a mixing bowl, completely blend the cheese and the butter. Add the Tabasco and Worcestershire sauces and mix well. Stir in the flour until it is thoroughly combined.

Scoop up about 1 teaspoon of the dough and flatten it with your fingers. Then wrap the flattened dough around an olive, enclosing the olive completely. Place each olive ball as it is completed on an ungreased baking sheet. When all the olive balls are made, bake them for 15 to 20 minutes, or until they are light brown. Serve hot or at room temperature.

Yield: about 45 Olive-Cheese Balls; 10 servings.

Cheese Straws

When I was in high school, I had a catering service for about two years. These Cheese Straws were one of the most popular of my party appetizers. They freeze very well.

2¼   cups unbleached white flour
½   teaspoon salt
1   teaspoon cayenne pepper, or to taste (The degree of hotness is determined by the amount of cayenne pepper added. The seasoning tends to be slightly milder after the dough has been baked.)
8   ounces sharp Cheddar cheese, grated
10   tablespoons butter or margarine, melted
1   teaspoon vegetable oil

In a large bowl, mix 2 cups of the flour together with the salt, cayenne pepper, and cheese. Add the melted butter and mix thoroughly. Cover the bowl and refrigerate the dough for 20 minutes.

Preheat the oven to 400 degrees.

Sprinkle the remaining ¼ cup of flour on a large pastry board. Transfer the dough from the bowl to the floured board. Flatten the dough slightly. Place a large piece of wax paper on top of the dough and roll the dough out to a ¼-inch thickness. Remove the wax paper.

Holding a table fork upside down, make ridges in the dough by drawing the prongs of the fork along the dough. Then cut the dough into 3- by 1-inch rectangles.

Grease a baking sheet with the oil and transfer the Cheese Straws to the baking sheet. Bake for 10 to 12 minutes, or until the Cheese Straws look dry, but are not brown. Transfer to a counter top to cool. Repeat with the remaining dough. Serve at room temperature.

Yield: 7 dozen Cheese Straws; 10 servings.

Wilder's Cheese Brioche

My cousin Wilder lives up to her name in every sense of the word. The name would be even more appropriate if she were called "Wildest." This cheese brioche is one of her specialties and it suits her perfectly, as it also has a hot pepper kick. As a party appetizer, it sparks the desire for more drinks and prepares the palate for the spicier foods to come. You can adjust the degree of hotness by using more or less cayenne pepper.

1	cup water
¼	cup butter or margarine
1	teaspoon salt
1	teaspoon cayenne pepper, or to taste
1	cup unbleached white flour, sifted
3	eggs
3	ounces Gruyère cheese, finely diced

Put the water, butter, salt, and cayenne pepper into a 1-quart saucepan. Bring to a boil over low heat. When the butter has melted, lower the heat and add the flour all at once, stirring with a wooden spoon until the dough forms a ball. Cook, stirring constantly, for 2 to 3 minutes, scraping the bottom of the pan often to keep the dough from sticking. Remove from the heat and transfer the dough to a large mixing bowl. Spread the dough out in the bowl and let it cool for 10 minutes.

Preheat the oven to 375 degrees. Grease a large baking sheet and set it aside.

When the dough is cool enough to handle, add all of the eggs and mix them in with your hand until they are completely incorporated. Add the cheese and mix it in thoroughly.

Gather the dough into a ball and place it in the center of the baking sheet. Spread the dough from the center of the ball to form a 5- by 8-inch oval.

Transfer the baking sheet to the oven and bake for 30 to 35 minutes, or until the brioche is light golden brown and puffy.

Transfer the brioche from the baking sheet to a cutting board. The brioche will deflate. Cut into 1- or 2-inch slices. Serve hot or at room temperature.

Yield: 16 slices; 4 servings.

Trout Pâté

Stage 1

2	10-ounce trout fillets
½	cup dry white wine
2	tablespoons apple cider vinegar
1	lemon, thinly sliced and seeded
1	small onion, thinly sliced
4	whole cloves
¼	teaspoon cayenne pepper
½	teaspoon fresh lemon juice
½	teaspoon Worcestershire sauce

Stage 2

1	pound trout fillets
¼	cup unbleached white flour
2	egg yolks
½	cup milk
2	tablespoons Cognac
2	egg whites
6	tablespoons butter or margarine at room temperature
1	teaspoon salt
½	teaspoon ground black pepper
1½	teaspoons fresh lemon juice
¼	teaspoon cayenne pepper
1	teaspoon Worcestershire sauce
2	tablespoons chopped pecans

For the Baking Dish

½	pound lean sliced bacon
1	lemon, thinly sliced and seeded

Garnish

½	cup Mayonnaise (page 111)
1	teaspoon dried tarragon
1	pound saltine crackers

To prepare Stage 1, place the trout fillets in a shallow baking dish. Add the remaining ingredients for Stage 1 and stir lightly. Cover and refrigerate overnight.

To prepare Stage 2, put the 1 pound of trout fillets in a bowl and mash, using a fork or your hand. Add the remaining ingredients for Stage 2 to the mashed trout and blend thoroughly.

To bake, preheat the oven to 300 degrees. Remove the marinated trout fillets from the refrigerator. Set the trout fillets aside and discard the marinade.

Line a 9- by 5- by 3-inch baking dish with the bacon strips. Let the strips hang over the edges of the dish. Place the lemon slices on the bottom and along the sides of the dish on top of the bacon.

Spread one third of the mixture from Stage 2 on top of the lemon slices. Lay over that 1 whole marinated trout fillet. Spread another third of the mixture over the fillet. Add the remaining marinated fillet and cover with the rest of the Stage 2 mixture. Fold the overhanging bacon strips over the top of the pâté.

Place the baking dish in a larger roasting pan and pour enough hot water into the roasting pan to come halfway up the sides of the baking dish. Bake for 2½ to 3 hours. If necessary, add more water to the roasting pan.

Remove the pâté from the oven and put the baking dish on a wire rack. Let the pâté cool to room temperature. Drain off any excess juices and remove the pâté from the baking dish. Remove all of the bacon and set it aside for another use.

To serve, mix the Mayonnaise and the tarragon together in a small bowl. Place the room-temperature pâté on a serving platter and cut it into slices. Lay the crackers next to the pâté. The pâté is eaten on a cracker, topped with a dab of Mayonnaise. It can also be refrigerated and served cold.

Yield: 8 servings.

Pâté in Crust

1	pound boneless chicken breast, cut into thin strips
½	cup brandy
1½	pounds ground lean pork

¼   teaspoon salt
¼   teaspoon ground black pepper
1   recipe Plain Pastry (page 143)
6   ounces cooked ham, cut into long narrow strips
1   egg
½   pound crackers

Put the chicken strips into a small mixing bowl and add half the brandy. Toss to thoroughly coat the chicken with the brandy. Marinate at room temperature for 2 to 3 hours.

Put the ground pork, salt, and pepper into another bowl. Add the remaining brandy and mix to combine well. Set aside until needed.

When the chicken has marinated, prepare the pastry. Roll out half of the pastry on a floured pastry board to a ⅛-inch thickness. Line the bottom and sides of a loaf pan with the rolled-out pastry, leaving a ½-inch overhang of dough all around the pan.

Spread half of the pork mixture over the dough on the bottom of the pan. Lay all of the marinated chicken strips over the pork mixture. Then pour on the marinade from the chicken. Make a layer of all of the ham strips on top of the chicken. Cover the ham with the remaining pork mixture.

Preheat the oven to 350 degrees.

Roll out half of the remaining pastry to a ⅛-inch thickness. (Store the remaining pastry in the refrigerator for another use.) Lay the rolled-out pastry on top of the pork mixture in the loaf pan. Turn up the overhanging edges of the dough and crimp both layers of dough together to seal them.

Beat the egg and brush the top of the pastry with the beaten egg. Cut two ½-inch-wide holes in the top crust and insert aluminum foil cones to allow heat to escape during baking.

Place the loaf pan on a baking sheet and transfer it to the oven. Bake for about 1½ hours. If the top crust begins to brown too quickly, cover it with aluminum foil.

Remove the pâté from the oven and drain off any juices. Gently remove the pâté from the loaf pan and transfer it to a serving platter. The pâté may be served hot or at room temperature, accompanied by crackers.

Yield: 8 servings.

Bayou Pâté

1	tablespoon butter or margarine
1	pound chicken livers
½	pound lean bacon slices
1	large onion, minced
1	tablespoon minced fresh dill
1	tablespoon minced fresh chives
1	tablespoon minced fresh parsley leaves
1	egg
2	tablespoons Cognac
2	garlic cloves, minced
10	ounces unsalted slab bacon, sliced ⅛ inch thick
½	pound crackers

Melt the butter in a large skillet. Add the chicken livers and fry them until they are thoroughly cooked. Transfer the livers to a large bowl and mash them with a fork until they are almost a paste.

Cook the bacon slices in the skillet until they are well done. Drain them on paper towels or a brown paper bag.

Crumble the bacon and add it to the livers with the onion, dill, chives, parsley, egg, Cognac, and garlic. Mix well.

Preheat the oven to 350 degrees.

Cook the slices of slab bacon until they are half done. Line a casserole or loaf pan with the bacon, saving a few slices for the top of the pâté. Pour all of the pâté mixture into the casserole and lay the reserved bacon slices on top. Cover the casserole and place it in a larger baking pan. Pour enough water into the baking pan to come halfway up the sides of the casserole.

Transfer the baking pan and casserole to the oven and bake for 1 hour. Remove from the oven and carefully drain any juices from the casserole. Remove the bacon slices from the top and sides of the pâté and let the pâté cool for a few hours. Serve accompanied by crackers.

Yield: 8 servings.

Grand-Mère's Daube Glacé

My grandmother served Daube Glacé on Sunday nights, when friends came over to listen to my grandfather's symphony and opera records. Good food always accompanied the good music. This recipe takes two days to prepare. It is often given as a present, or served at special occasions.

Day 1

2	tablespoons bacon drippings
4	pounds boneless beef eye round (about 4 inches thick)
1	sweet green pepper, sliced
1	sweet red pepper, sliced
1	teaspoon salt
1	teaspoon cayenne pepper
1	teaspoon ground black pepper

Day 2

1	teaspoon vegetable oil
2	loin pork chops
2	to 3 cups water
1	large carrot, peeled
3	medium-sized onions, peeled but left whole
2	to 3 garlic cloves, minced
2	bay leaves
¼	teaspoon dried thyme
¼	teaspoon ground cloves
2	lemons, cut into ⅛-inch-thick slices and seeded
½	teaspoon salt
½	teaspoon ground black pepper
1	to 2 10¾-ounce cans beef bouillon
1	tablespoon dry sherry
2	¼-ounce packages unflavored gelatin
2	tablespoons cold water
1	2½-ounce can pitted black olives, drained and sliced
½	cup Mayonnaise (page 111)
6	to 8 sprigs fresh parsley, washed and dried
½	pound saltine crackers

Day 1: In a large skillet, heat the bacon drippings and add the meat. Brown the meat on all sides. Then add the sliced peppers and cook until they are tender. Transfer the meat and peppers to a bowl. Sprinkle the salt, cayenne pepper, and black pepper over the meat to coat it on all sides. Cover the bowl and refrigerate for 24 hours.

Day 2: Heat the oil in a large pot. Add the pork chops and brown them on all sides over medium heat. Add the beef and peppers from Day 1, along with the water. Bring to a boil, lower the heat, cover, and simmer for 30 minutes.

Add the carrot, onions, garlic, bay leaves, thyme, cloves, lemons, salt, and pepper. Simmer over low heat, stirring occasionally and turning the meat every 30 minutes until it is tender. After the first 30 minutes, add 1 can of beef bouillon and more water if necessary, to keep the meat covered with liquid. The meat should be tender after 1½ hours. Remove the beef and pork and let them cool. Reserve the broth and vegetables.

Pull the meat into long thin shreds. Discard the fat and bones.

Remove the lemon slices and carrot from the broth. Set the lemon slices aside and cut the carrot into ⅛-inch-thick rounds. Strain the remaining broth into a bowl, discarding any solids. There should be about 4 cups of broth; if not, add beef bouillon to make that amount. Add the sherry to the broth, and heat the mixture slightly.

Soften the gelatin in the 2 tablespoons of cold water. Add the gelatin to the broth, stirring until it is completely dissolved.

Lay one quarter of the shredded meat in the bottom of each of two loaf pans. Then distribute the sliced lemon, carrot, and olives over the meat. Lay the remaining shredded meat equally over the vegetables. Pour equal amounts of the broth into each loaf pan. The Daube Glacé should be about ¾ inch thick. Allow the mixture to cool in the pans; then cover and refrigerate for 3 to 4 hours, or until the Daube is set.

To serve, fill the kitchen sink with a few inches of hot water. Dip the pans into the hot water for 30 to 60 seconds. Dry the pans off and invert them onto a large serving platter. Spread a thin layer of Mayonnaise over the top and sides of the Daube and decorate the sides with the parsley sprigs. Cut the Daube into bite-sized pieces and serve with the crackers.

Yield: 8 servings.

Fried Oysters Wrapped in Bacon

1   dozen fresh oysters, shucked
¼   cup oyster liquor
1   bay leaf
1   teaspoon Worcestershire sauce
4   slices (about ½ ounce each) lean bacon
½   cup unbleached white flour
2   eggs
1   cup unseasoned dry bread crumbs (see Note)
2   cups vegetable oil

Put the oysters, oyster liquor, bay leaf, and Worcestershire sauce into a 1-quart saucepan. Poach the oysters over medium heat until the edges of the oysters begin to curl, about 2 minutes. Remove the oysters from the liquid and set them aside. Discard the liquid.

Cut the bacon slices into thirds. Wrap each oyster with a piece of bacon, securing it with a toothpick.

Spread the flour on a piece of wax paper. Beat the eggs in a small bowl. Spread the bread crumbs on a piece of wax paper.

Dip each bacon-wrapped oyster first in the flour and then in the beaten egg. Then roll each one in the bread crumbs to coat it completely.

Heat the oil in a 9-inch skillet. When the oil is very hot, lower the heat and add the oysters to the skillet. Fry them for 5 minutes, turning once, or until they are golden brown. Drain the oysters on paper towels or a brown paper bag and serve immediately.

Yield: 4 servings.

Note: To prepare your own bread crumbs, store leftover bread in a paper bag at room temperature for 2 to 3 weeks, or until it is very hard and stale. Then put the bread in the container of a blender and process for 30 to 40 seconds, or until it is finely ground. Store the bread crumbs in an airtight container at room temperature.

Oysters Rockefeller

2	10-ounce packages frozen spinach
4	scallions, coarsely chopped
2	large celery stalks, coarsely chopped
¼	bunch parsley, coarsely chopped
¼	head iceberg lettuce, coarsely chopped
1	tablespoon Worcestershire sauce
2	teaspoons anchovy paste, or 4 anchovy fillets, mashed
½	teaspoon salt
½	teaspoon Tabasco sauce
1	teaspoon aniseeds
1	cup unseasoned dry bread crumbs
4	to 5 pounds rock salt
24	fresh oysters, shucked, rinsed, and drained

Put the spinach in a steamer basket and steam over boiling water for about 5 minutes. Transfer the spinach to a colander and let it drain thoroughly.

Put the drained spinach into the container of a blender and purée it. (This may have to be done in two batches.) Transfer the puréed spinach to a bowl.

Put the scallions, celery, parsley, and lettuce into the container of the blender and process until the mixture is puréed. Transfer to the bowl with the spinach and blend thoroughly.

Return all of the puréed mixture to the container of the blender and add the Worcestershire sauce, anchovy paste, salt, Tabasco sauce, and aniseeds. Blend for 1 minute on medium speed. Transfer the mixture to a bowl and stir in the bread crumbs, mixing them in thoroughly. Set aside until needed.

Preheat the oven to 400 degrees.

Spread enough rock salt to cover the bottom of each of six 6-inch pie pans. Place 4 oyster shells in each pie pan on top of the rock salt. Place 1 oyster in each shell. Bake the oysters for 5 minutes. The oysters should look a little dry.

Remove the pie pans from the oven and cover each oyster completely with the reserved sauce, using about 3 tablespoons for each oyster. Return the oysters to the oven and bake for 15 to 20 minutes, or until the tops are browned.

Serve directly from the oven, putting the pie pans on individual heatproof dinner plates.
Yield: 6 servings.

Note: If you do not have the individual pie pans, you can bake the oysters in a jelly roll pan.

Crab Quiche

7½ ounces fresh lump crab meat, shells and cartilage removed
1 9-inch pastry shell (see Plain Pastry, page 143)
3 ounces Swiss cheese, grated
4 eggs, beaten
1½ cups light cream
⅓ cup minced onion
1 teaspoon salt
¼ teaspoon cayenne pepper
1 tablespoon chopped fresh parsley leaves

Preheat the oven to 425 degrees.

Sprinkle the crab meat over the bottom of the pastry shell. Then sprinkle the grated cheese over the crab meat.

Put the eggs, cream, onion, salt, and cayenne pepper into a bowl. Beat until well blended and then pour the mixture over the crab meat and cheese in the pastry shell. Sprinkle the parsley over all.

Transfer the pie pan to a baking sheet and bake on the middle rack of the oven for 15 minutes. Lower the oven temperature to 300 degrees and bake for 30 minutes longer, or until a knife inserted near the center comes out clean. Remove the quiche from the oven and let it cool for 10 minutes before slicing it.
Yield: 6 servings.

Shrimp Rémoulade

Shrimp Rémoulade is usually served as a first course. Rémoulade Sauce is excellent with lump crab meat, stuffed tomatoes, avocados, or lettuce, or as a dip for raw vegetables. It is best when made at least one day in advance.

Sauce

2	tablespoons bottled horseradish
½	celery stalk, chopped
2	scallions, chopped
¼	cup chopped fresh parsley leaves
⅓	cup fresh lemon juice
¼	cup paprika
9	ounces Creole mustard or spicy mustard
¼	teaspoon salt
¼	teaspoon ground black pepper
1	garlic clove
⅓	cup olive oil

Boiled Shrimp Seasonings

2	quarts water
1	lemon, cut into quarters
1	cup chopped celery tops
2	garlic cloves, halved
1	teaspoon salt
½	teaspoon cayenne pepper
2	bay leaves

Shrimp

80	large fresh shrimp
1½	pounds Bibb lettuce, washed and dried

To prepare the sauce, put the horseradish, celery, scallions, parsley, lemon juice, paprika, mustard, salt, black pepper, and garlic into the container of a blender. With the machine running on medium speed, slowly pour in the olive oil. When all the olive oil has been added, blend for 1 minute longer. Pour the sauce into a jar with a tight-fitting lid and store in the refrigerator. The sauce will keep for weeks.

To prepare the shrimp, put the water and seasonings in a 4-quart pot and bring to a boil. Lower the heat, cover, and simmer for 10 minutes. Add the raw shrimp and cook for 5 minutes. Drain the shrimp in a colander. When the shrimp are cool enough to handle, peel and devein them. Set the shrimp aside.

Pour the Rémoulade Sauce into a large bowl. Add the shrimp and toss to thoroughly coat the shrimp with the sauce. For best results, cover and marinate the shrimp in the sauce overnight in the refrigerator.

To serve, make a bed of lettuce on individual salad dishes. Place 8 marinated shrimp on top of the lettuce. Pour any extra sauce on top of the shrimp.

Yield: 10 servings.

Variation
For Crab Meat Rémoulade, substitute 4 pounds of lump crab meat for the shrimp.

Barbecued Shrimp

These shrimp are usually served as a first course. They are finger-licking good.

    1   pound medium-sized fresh raw shrimp in the shell
    2   teaspoons cayenne pepper
    4   tablespoons butter or margarine

Preheat the oven to 350 degrees.

Spread the shrimp in an even layer in a jelly roll pan. Sprinkle the shrimp with the cayenne pepper and dot them with pieces of the butter.

Bake for 5 minutes and stir the shrimp to thoroughly coat them with the butter. Return to the oven and bake for 5 minutes longer; then stir again. Bake for 5 minutes more and remove from the oven. Serve immediately.

Yield: 4 servings.

Toasted Pecans

When we were children, my mother would hide the toasted pecans from us until the beginning of a party. However, that didn't really help much, because as soon as the pecans were served, we would swoop down on the bowl and eat them in minutes.

    ¼   cup butter or margarine
    ½   pound shelled pecan halves
    ¼   teaspoon salt

Preheat the oven to 350 degrees.

Melt the butter in a saucepan. Then add the pecan halves and stir until they are thoroughly coated.

Spread the pecans on a jelly roll pan and bake, stirring once, for 15 to 20 minutes, or until they are lightly toasted. Remove from the oven and sprinkle with the salt. Let cool to room temperature before serving. The pecans can be stored in an airtight container.

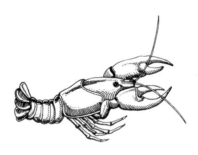

SOUPS & STEWS

In the past, soup was a part of every dinner.
Prepared each day, it was a wonderful interlude from
the first course to the main dish. Today, eating habits
have changed. Soups, such as gumbo, bisque, or
étouffée, are usually the main course and are served
with fresh French bread. Of course a small bowl of
soup can be served before the main course, but it is
hard to have just a little.

Gazpacho

This soup tastes best when it's made a day or two before you serve it.

Soup

    4   large ripe tomatoes, peeled and seeded
    1   large cucumber, washed and seeded
    1   sweet green pepper, washed and seeded
    3   tablespoons fresh lemon juice
    2   large onions, chopped
   8½   cups tomato juice
    ½   teaspoon salt
    ½   teaspoon ground black pepper
    ¼   cup olive oil
    ¼   cup apple cider vinegar

Garnish

    1   cup Croutons (page 125)
    2   medium-sized ripe tomatoes, seeded and diced
    2   medium-sized cucumbers, seeded and diced

Put batches of the soup ingredients into the container of a blender and process on medium speed until they are chopped and well blended. Transfer to a bowl, cover, and refrigerate.

Serve the soup cold with the garnishes on the side.

Yield: 8 servings.

Vegetable Soup

Many people find that making vegetable soup can be therapeutic. The chopping of the vegetables and the delicious aroma during the long, slow simmering soothe the soul.

My father likes to add matzo balls to the soup or to sprinkle crumbled crackers on top of his serving.

This soup tastes best when it is made a day ahead. It also freezes very well.

2   pounds lean beef brisket
1   ½-pound beef soup bone
1   large onion, cut in half
2   celery stalks, cut in half
1   large potato, cut in half
1   teaspoon salt
3   quarts cold water
1   12-ounce can tomato paste, or 4 large ripe tomatoes,
      peeled, seeded, and quartered
½   medium-sized head cabbage, finely chopped or grated
5   celery stalks, minced
1   large onion, minced
1   medium-sized potato, peeled and minced
1   sweet green pepper, seeded and minced
3   large carrots, minced
1   medium-sized turnip, peeled and diced
6   sprigs fresh parsley, minced
1   teaspoon ground black pepper
¼   teaspoon cayenne pepper
     Kernels from 3 ears of fresh corn
½   pound fresh string beans, trimmed and cut into
      1-inch-long pieces
1   cup frozen green peas
¼   pound vermicelli or spaghettini

Combine the brisket, soup bone, halved onion, celery, large
potato, salt, and cold water in a large pot. Bring to a boil, lower
the heat, cover, and simmer for 3 hours. Then remove the brisket, bone, onion, celery, and potato. Set the broth aside.

Discard the soup bone and cut the brisket into bite-sized
pieces, discarding any fat. Return the meat to the broth. (Alter-
nately, you can save the meat for Soup Meat Salad, page 100.)
Mash the onion, celery, and potato through a strainer and return
the purée to the broth.

Add all the remaining ingredients, except the vermicelli, to
the soup mixture. Bring to a boil and simmer, partially covered,
for 3 to 4 hours. If necessary, add 1 or 2 cups of water to prevent
the soup from becoming too thick.

Add the vermicelli to the simmering soup 10 to 15 minutes
before you serve it.
        Yield: 10 servings.

Red Bean Soup

8	cups drained cooked Red Beans (page 88)
2	cups water
2	cups milk
2	teaspoons salt
½	teaspoon ground black pepper
3	tablespoons minced onion
½	teaspoon Tabasco sauce
1	cup Croutons (page 125), optional

Put the beans, in batches, in the container of a blender and process until they are puréed. Then put the purée into a heavy 3-quart pot. Add the water, milk, salt, pepper, onion, and Tabasco sauce. Mix thoroughly. Simmer over low heat for 20 minutes, stirring occasionally to keep the soup from sticking to the bottom of the pot. If the soup is too thick, add ½ cup of water. Serve in individual soup bowls with the Croutons sprinkled on top, if desired.

Yield: 6 servings.

Crawfish Bisque

I once made five gallons of this bisque as a gift to friends who were getting married. It was a forty-hour labor of love, which was thoroughly enjoyed by everyone at their wedding reception.

Seafood

12   pounds crawfish (see Note)

Stuffing for the Crawfish Heads

¼   cup vegetable oil
1   cup unbleached white flour
1   large onion, minced
½   large sweet green pepper, minced
2   cups crawfish fat, or 2 cups milk
½   cup canned tomato sauce
2½   cups chopped crawfish tails (from the crawfish above)
2   teaspoons salt
½   teaspoon ground black pepper
¾   teaspoon cayenne pepper
1   cup unseasoned dry bread crumbs
2   tablespoons chopped fresh parsley leaves
½   cup butter or margarine, melted

Bisque

½   cup vegetable oil
1   cup unbleached white flour
1   large onion, minced
1   large sweet green pepper, minced
½   cup crawfish fat (optional)
12   cups water
4   teaspoons salt
1½   teaspoons cayenne pepper
½   cup canned tomato sauce
2   garlic cloves, minced
2   to 3 cups crawfish tails (from crawfish above)
3   tablespoons minced fresh parsley leaves

To Serve

4   to 5 cups hot Steamed Rice (page 76)

To prepare the crawfish, remove and clean the shells from 50 crawfish heads. Reserve the head shells. Remove the tail meat and discard the crawfish tail shells. Devein the tail meat and set it aside.

To prepare the stuffing for the crawfish heads, mix the oil with ½ cup of the flour in a heavy pot. Cook, stirring constantly, over medium heat until the roux turns light brown. Add the onion and green pepper and cook until the vegetables are soft. Add the crawfish fat, tomato sauce, and chopped crawfish tails and mix well. Season with the salt, black pepper, and cayenne pepper. Simmer, uncovered, over low heat for 15 minutes. Add the bread crumbs and mix well. Stir in the parsley and butter and remove the pot from the stove. Use 1 or 2 tablespoons of the stuffing to fill each crawfish head shell.

Preheat the oven to 300 degrees.

Spread the remaining ½ cup of flour on a sheet of wax paper. Roll the stuffed crawfish heads in the flour and put them on ungreased baking sheets. When all the crawfish heads have been floured, bake them for 15 minutes. Remove from the oven and set aside.

To prepare the bisque, make a roux by mixing the oil with the flour in a heavy pot over medium heat. Cook, stirring constantly with a wooden spoon, over medium heat until it bubbles and turns light brown. Add the onion and green pepper and cook until the vegetables are soft. Add the crawfish fat, water, salt, cayenne, and tomato sauce. Simmer, uncovered, over low heat for 30 minutes. Add the garlic and simmer for 10 minutes longer. Add the crawfish tails and simmer for 5 minutes. Add the parsley and 1 to 2 cups of water, if necessary. Stir well to combine.

To serve, add the baked stuffed crawfish heads to the bisque and bring to a simmer. Cook over low heat for 10 minutes. Then put ½ cup of the hot rice into each large soup bowl and pour on the hot bisque, including 5 or 6 stuffed crawfish heads in each serving. To eat, scoop the stuffing out of the crawfish heads with a soup spoon and eat the stuffing with the rice and bisque.

Yield: 10 servings.

Note: If boiled crawfish are not available use 5 cups (about 2 pounds raw peeled) ''store-bought'' crawfish tails and 50 cleaned ''store-bought'' crawfish head shells.

Seafood Gumbo

1	tablespoon vegetable oil
2	10-ounce packages frozen cut okra
2	medium-sized onions, minced
3	celery stalks, minced
8	cups water
1	6-ounce can tomato paste
1	teaspoon salt
1	teaspoon ground black pepper
½	pound fresh lump crab meat
1	pound large fresh shrimp, peeled and deveined
4	cups hot Steamed Rice (page 76)

Heat the oil in a 4-quart pot. Add the okra, onions, and celery. Simmer over medium heat for 30 minutes, stirring occasionally and lowering the heat, if necessary, to prevent the mixture from sticking to the bottom of the pot. The okra should be very gooey.

Add the water, tomato paste, salt, and pepper. Bring to a boil, cover, and cook over medium-high heat for 30 minutes. Lower the heat and simmer, covered, for 2 to 3 hours, or until the okra has almost dissolved. Stir occasionally. If the soup gets too thick, add 1 or 2 cups more water.

Add the crab meat and simmer over low heat for 10 minutes. Add shrimp and simmer for 5 minutes. Taste for seasoning, and add more black pepper, if desired.

To serve, spoon ½ cup of hot rice into large individual soup bowls. Fill the bowls with heaping portions of the hot seafood and gumbo. Serve with hot French bread on the side.

Yield: 8 servings.

Variation

For Chicken and Sausage Gumbo, substitute 1 pound of mild sausage (cut into 1-inch-thick pieces and cooked in a skillet and drained) and 1 pound of boneless chicken breast (cut into 1-inch-pieces) for the shrimp and crab meat. Add the sausage and chicken breast cubes at the time you would have added the shrimp and crab meat above.

Turkey Gumbo

2	tablespoons vegetable oil
2	tablespoons unbleached white flour
½	cup chopped onion
2	celery stalks and tops, coarsely chopped
1	garlic clove, quartered
14	cups water
1	carcass from a 12-pound turkey
1	cup chopped turkey meat
1	cup Steamed Rice (page 76)
1	teaspoon chopped fresh parsley leaves
¼	to ½ teaspoon salt
¼	to ½ teaspoon ground black pepper

Heat the oil over medium heat in an 8-quart pot. Add the flour and cook, stirring constantly with a wooden spoon, until the mixture is smooth and light brown. Add the onion, celery, and garlic, and sauté over low heat for about 10 minutes, or until the vegetables are tender.

Add 12 cups of the water and the turkey carcass to the pot. Bring to a boil, lower the heat, and simmer, uncovered, for 3½ hours, stirring occasionally. If the broth boils down too much, add 2 more cups water.

Pour the broth through a strainer into a bowl and let it cool. Reserve the meat from the carcass and chop it into small pieces. Add it to the 1 cup of turkey meat. Discard the carcass and vegetables from the broth.

Refrigerate the broth for 2 hours, or until the fat rises to the top. Skim off and discard the fat. Pour the broth into a 3-quart pot. Add the turkey meat, rice, parsley, salt, and pepper. Cover and simmer for 5 minutes, or until heated through.

Yield: 4 servings.

Variation

If you wish, 4 ounces of vermicelli, cooked *al dente,* can be substituted for the rice.

Aunt Lulu's Shrimp Étouffée

¼ cup vegetable oil
¼ cup unbleached white flour
4 shallots, minced
2 celery stalks, minced
½ cup minced fresh parsley leaves
4 cups water
½ teaspoon salt
1 teaspoon ground black pepper
2 tablespoons tomato paste
1 tablespoon Kitchen Bouquet
4 pounds large fresh shrimp, peeled and deveined
5 cups hot Steamed Rice (page 76)

Heat the oil in a heavy 4-quart pot. Add the flour and cook over medium heat, stirring constantly with a wooden spoon, until the mixture is light brown. Add the shallots, celery, and parsley and sauté for 7 minutes, or until the vegetables are tender. Stir frequently. Lower the heat to a simmer, cover, and cook for 5 minutes longer.

Add the water, salt, pepper, tomato paste, and Kitchen Bouquet. Cover and simmer for 15 minutes. Add the shrimp and simmer for 5 minutes. Do not overcook the shrimp.

To serve, spoon ½ to ⅔ cup hot rice into individual large soup bowls. Pour heaping spoonfuls of the hot étouffée over the rice.

Yield: 6 servings.

Crawfish Étouffée

1	pound crawfish tails, peeled and deveined
1	teaspoon salt
¼	teaspoon ground black pepper
¼	teaspoon cayenne pepper
1	tablespoon butter or margarine
2	medium-sized onions, minced
1	large sweet green pepper, minced
2	celery stalks, minced
4	garlic cloves, minced
2	ounces crawfish fat (optional)
2	to 3 cups warm water
1	to 2 tablespoons cornstarch dissolved in ¼ cup cold water
1	scallion, minced
2	tablespoons minced fresh parsley leaves
2	cups hot Steamed Rice (page 76)

Put the crawfish tails into a medium-sized bowl and season them with the salt, black pepper, and cayenne pepper. Set aside until needed.

Melt the butter in a large heavy pot. Add the onions, green pepper, celery, and garlic and sauté over low heat until the vegetables are very tender. Add the crawfish fat, if used, and 2 cups of the water. Bring to a boil. Lower the heat, cover, and simmer over low heat for 15 minutes.

Slowly add the cornstarch mixture to the pot, stirring constantly. Taste for seasoning, and add more salt and pepper, if necessary. Add the scallion, parsley, and the seasoned crawfish tails to the pot, adding more water, if necessary, to submerge the tails. Return to a boil and lower the heat. Cover and simmer over low heat for 10 minutes. Remove the étouffée from the heat and let it stand, covered, for a few minutes. Serve in large soup bowls, pouring the étouffée over ½-cup servings of hot rice.

Yield: 4 servings.

Tatee's Oyster Stew

Almost every Southerner has a nickname. My grandmother Lottie, whose real name was Charlotte, was also called Tatee. She always said, "Anybody who can read, can cook." This is partially true, but it is also a matter of timing and knowing how to get all of the dishes for a meal on the table at the same time.

This oyster stew was one of her favorite dishes.

1	tablespoon butter or margarine
6	shallots, minced
1	tablespoon unbleached white flour
24	fresh oysters, shucked (Reserve the oyster liquor.)
¼	to ½ cup water
4	cups milk
½	teaspoon dried thyme
1	garlic clove, minced
1	tablespoon chopped fresh parsley leaves
¼	teaspoon salt
¼	teaspoon ground black pepper

Melt the butter in a large heavy pot. Add the shallots and sauté until they are tender. Sprinkle the flour over the shallots and stir well. Then add the remaining ingredients and simmer, uncovered, for 20 minutes. Do not let the stew boil. Serve in large bowls.

Yield: 4 servings.

EGGS, CHEESE & LUNCHEON DISHES

You can walk in the French Quarter (or "the Quarter," as it is called by locals) and see people on their wrought-iron balconies, watching the parade passing on the street. Behind the houses there are old brick courtyards with small gardens. Many of these gardens have banana, magnolia, or palmetto trees, plus gardenia or azalea bushes, and are lined with bird of paradise, elephant ear, and bamboo plants. After a cooling summer rain, you can sit in the courtyard, sip a refreshing cold drink, and enjoy a light delicious lunch.

Eggs Sardou

---

    2   10-ounce packages frozen chopped spinach
    1   tablespoon butter or margarine
   ¼   teaspoon ground black pepper
    2   6-ounce jars marinated artichoke hearts
    4   whole wheat English muffins, halved
    6   to 8 cups water
   ½   cup apple cider vinegar
    8   eggs
    1   cup Hollandaise Sauce (page 108) at room
        temperature
   ¼   teaspoon paprika

Preheat the oven to 250 degrees.

Put the spinach in a steamer basket and steam over boiling water for about 5 minutes, or until it is just soft. Transfer the spinach to a colander and let it drain thoroughly. Turn the drained spinach into a small casserole. Season it with the butter and pepper, cover the casserole, and place it in the oven.

Cut the artichoke hearts into quarters and put them in a small casserole. Pour the marinade from the jars over the artichokes. Cover the casserole and place it in the oven.

Toast the muffin halves lightly; then transfer them to a pie pan and keep them warm in the oven. (You can also heat your oven-proof serving plates at this time.)

Pour 3½ to 4 cups of water into two 8-inch skillets. Add ¼ cup vinegar to each skillet. Bring the water and vinegar to a boil. Place a folded clean dish towel on the counter near the stove.

When the water and vinegar mixture has come to a boil, break each egg into a cup, one at a time, and slide 4 eggs into each skillet. Keep the liquid in the skillets at a constant medium boil, and cook the eggs for 2 to 4 minutes, or until the whites are firm but the yolks are still runny. Use a large slotted spoon to scoop the eggs from the skillets. Let the eggs drain on the dish towel.

To serve, place 2 muffin halves on each hot plate. Spoon 2 to 3 tablespoons of hot spinach over each muffin half. Top the spinach with equal amounts of the drained artichoke hearts. Place a poached egg on top of each muffin half. Pour a few tablespoons of the Hollandaise Sauce over each egg. Sprinkle with paprika and serve immediately.

Yield: 4 servings.

Corn Pudding Soufflé

This soufflé is a good accompaniment to meat dishes. It tastes best when it is made with fresh, sweet white corn.

Kernels from 6 ears fresh white corn (If white corn is not available, you can use yellow corn.)
3   tablespoons butter or margarine, melted
3   egg yolks
1   cup milk
1   teaspoon salt
½   teaspoon baking powder
3   tablespoons unbleached white flour
3   egg whites
½   teaspoon oil

Preheat the oven to 325 degrees.

Grate the raw corn kernels in the container of a blender. Then pour them into a large mixing bowl. Add the butter, egg yolks, milk, salt, baking powder, and flour and mix thoroughly.

In a separate bowl, beat the egg whites until they are fluffy and firm. Gently fold the beaten egg whites into the corn mixture.

Grease a straight-sided 2-quart baking dish with the oil. Pour the soufflé mixture into the baking dish and bake for 50 minutes. Serve immediately.

Yield: 4 servings.

Papou's Cheese Soufflé

2   tablespoons plus ½ teaspoon butter or margarine
2   tablespoons plus ½ teaspoon unbleached white flour
1   cup milk
1   cup grated Gruyère or sharp Cheddar cheese
¼   teaspoon salt
¼   teaspoon ground black pepper
¼   teaspoon cayenne pepper
4   egg yolks at room temperature
5   egg whites at room temperature

Melt the 2 tablespoons of butter in a medium-sized saucepan and add the 2 tablespoons of flour all at once. Blend with a wooden spoon over medium heat until the mixture becomes foamy and the lumps have disappeared. Gradually stir in half of the milk. Cook and stir until the sauce thickens. Then gradually add the remaining milk, stirring constantly, and cook for 2 to 3 minutes. Add the cheese and stir constantly until the mixture thickens. Cook for 1 or 2 minutes longer, and season with the salt, black pepper, and cayenne pepper. Remove from the heat. Let the sauce cool for 20 minutes.

Preheat the oven to 400 degrees.

Stir the egg yolks into the sauce and mix thoroughly.

In a separate bowl, beat the egg whites until they are stiff. Gently fold the beaten egg whites into the cooled cheese sauce.

Use the remaining ½ teaspoon of butter to grease the bottom and sides of a straight-sided 1-quart baking dish. Dust the inside of the dish with the remaining ½ teaspoon flour. Pour the soufflé mixture into the baking dish and put the baking dish into the oven. Immediately lower the oven temperature to 375 degrees. Bake the soufflé for approximately 30 minutes, or until the top is golden brown. Serve immediately.

Yield: 4 servings.

Cheese Croquettes (Fried Cheese Balls)

1   pound sharp Cheddar cheese, grated
2   eggs, separated and at room temperature
½   teaspoon dry mustard
⅛   teaspoon cayenne pepper
1   tablespoon minced onion
¼   cup evaporated milk
⅓   cup unbleached white flour or cracker crumbs
1½   cups vegetable oil

In a large bowl, mix together the cheese, egg whites, dry mustard, cayenne pepper, and onion.

In a small bowl, mix together the egg yolks and evaporated milk. Spread the flour on a piece of wax paper.

Mold the cheese mixture into 8 croquettes (oval balls). Roll each croquette first in the egg yolk mixture, then in the flour, and then in the egg yolk mixture again. Place each completed croquette on a baking sheet as it is coated. Refrigerate the croquettes on the baking sheet for about 20 minutes, or until they are firm.

To fry the croquettes, heat the oil in a 6-inch cast-iron skillet over medium heat. When the oil is very hot, drop the croquettes into the skillet, one at a time, until the skillet is full. Do not crowd the croquettes. Fry the croquettes until they are brown on all sides, using a slotted spoon to roll the croquettes in the oil. Drain the croquettes on paper towels or a brown paper bag. Serve hot.

Yield: 4 servings.

Note: The croquettes can be kept hot in a 350-degree oven.

PO-BOYS

Po-Boys are an institution in New Orleans. They are one of the most popular luncheon specials and are usually served with a cold, frothy Barq's Root Beer or long-neck Dixie Beer. The secret to a great Po-Boy is fresh French bread. In New Orleans, fresh Po-Boy loaves are baked daily. If the loaves are not available in your area, use the freshest French bread you can find. The crust should be light and crisp and the inside of the bread soft.

Po-Boys are best when they are juicy and messy. They can be eaten in restaurants, at home, or on picnics. A Po-Boy, or a Po-Boy loaf, comes in a half-loaf portion or a whole-loaf portion. A half-loaf is about six inches long; a whole loaf is about twelve inches long. Typical Po-Boys are Fried Oyster, Fried Shrimp, Hot Roast Beef, Ham and Cheese, and Hot Sausage. They are dressed with lots of mayonnaise, shredded lettuce, sliced tomato, and a few sliced pickles. Ketchup, mustard, and Tartare Sauce are optional. Here are a few recipes for Po-Boys. Let your imagination create your own favorite combinations.

Fried Oyster Po-Boy

    8   ounces fresh French bread
    ⅓   cup Mayonnaise (page 111)
    ½   cup Tartare Sauce (page 111), optional
    2   ounces iceberg lettuce, thinly sliced
    ½   large ripe tomato, thinly sliced
    1   recipe Fried Oysters (page 69)
    ¼   teaspoon salt
    ¼   teaspoon ground black pepper
         Juice of 1 lemon
    ½   cup ketchup (optional)

Preheat the oven to 300 degrees.

Cut the bread in half to make 2 loaves. Then cut each loaf in half lengthwise. Put the bread on a baking sheet and heat in the oven for 3 minutes.

Put the warm bread on a cutting board. Spread each piece of bread with Mayonnaise and Tartare Sauce, if desired. Lay the lettuce and tomato on one half of the bread for each sandwich.

Place 12 hot oysters on the other piece of bread. Sprinkle the oysters with salt and pepper and squeeze lemon juice over all. If desired, top the oysters with some ketchup. Close the sandwich gently and cut it in half. Transfer to a plate and enjoy.

Yield: 2 servings.

Variation

To make a Fried Shrimp Po-Boy, substitute 1 recipe Fried Shrimp (page 69) for the oysters.

Hot Roast Beef Po-Boy

1	pound cooked Roast Beef (page 42), very thinly sliced
½	cup Roast Beef Gravy (page 42)
8	ounces fresh French bread
½	cup Mayonnaise (page 111)
2	ounces iceberg lettuce, thinly sliced
½	large ripe tomato, thinly sliced
8	slices dill pickle
¼	teaspoon salt
¼	teaspoon ground black pepper

Preheat the oven to 300 degrees.

In a saucepan, simmer the meat in the gravy over medium heat for 4 minutes. Turn the meat occasionally; it is done when it is completely brown.

Cut the bread in half to make 2 loaves. Then cut each loaf in half lengthwise. Put the bread on a baking sheet and heat in the oven for 3 minutes.

Put the warm bread on a cutting board. Spread each piece of bread with Mayonnaise. Lay the lettuce and tomato on one half of the bread for each sandwich. Lay 4 slices of pickle on top of each portion of tomato.

Lay half of the roast beef on the other piece of bread. Pour the gravy on top of the meat. Sprinkle with salt and pepper. Close the sandwich gently and cut it in half. Transfer to a plate and enjoy.

Yield: 2 servings.

MEATS

The rich Mississippi delta region of Louisiana has been called a "sportsman's paradise." It provides an abundance of fish, shellfish, and game. The hunter's bounty often consists of duck, quail, rabbit, snipe, partridge, deer, and squirrel. Drawing from the wealth of these fresh foods, Louisiana can also be called a "gourmet's paradise."

To make New Orleans cuisine readily available for cooks anywhere, the following recipes use beef, pork, or lamb. The simplicity of New Orleans home cooking is found in the roast recipes. The roasts are tasty in themselves, or they can be used in Po-Boys or Jambalaya. There are also traditional meat dishes such as Grillades, Glazed Pork Chops, and Beef Scallopini.

Roast Beef

1½   teaspoons salt
1½   teaspoons ground black pepper
1   3- to 4-pound bottom round roast beef
1   cup water

Gravy
¾   cup water
¼   teaspoon salt
¼   teaspoon ground black pepper

Preheat the oven to 350 degrees.

Mix the salt and pepper together in a small cup. Rub the mixture on all sides of the beef. Place the beef in a heavy roasting pan. Pour ½ cup of the water into the roasting pan. Bake for 1½ hours.

After the first hour, add the remaining ½ cup of water to the roasting pan. When done, the meat should be rare in the center. If desired, cook longer to reach the degree of doneness you wish.

Transfer the roast to a hot serving platter. Set the roasting pan with the juices aside.

To make the gravy, add the water, salt, and pepper to the pan juices. Scrape up the browned-on bits in the bottom of the pan with a spatula. Pour the gravy into a saucepan and heat for a few minutes over medium heat.

To serve, cut the roast beef into thin slices and pour the gravy over them.

         Yield: 6 servings.

Pépère's Beef Scallopini

My father frequently visits an old Italian restaurant in New Orleans. He loves to go into the kitchen and talk to the proprietor/chef. During one of his visits, he raved so much about the scallopini the restaurant serves that the proprietor gave him the family recipe.

  6 ounces fettuccini or noodles
  ¼ cup plus 2 tablespoons butter or margarine
  ⅓ cup chopped fresh parsley leaves
  1 pound beef round steak, cut into eight ⅜-inch-thick slices
  ½ teaspoon salt
  ½ teaspoon ground black pepper
  ½ cup unbleached white flour
  2 cups dry Marsala
  ¼ pound fresh mushrooms, washed and sliced
  ½ cup freshly grated Parmesan cheese

Preheat the oven to 350 degrees.

Cook the fettuccine, following the package directions, until it is *al dente*. Drain the pasta thoroughly and transfer it to a baking dish. Blend 2 tablespoons of the butter and the chopped parsley with the fettuccine. Toss to mix well. Cover the baking dish and place it in the oven to keep the pasta warm while you prepare the meat.

Gently pound the beef slices with a wooden rolling pin until they are approximately ¼ inch thick. Sprinkle the meat with salt and pepper.

Spread the flour on a piece of wax paper. Press the slices of beef into the flour to coat them on both sides.

Melt 2 tablespoons of the remaining butter in each of two large skillets over medium heat. Add the beef and cook for 2 to 3 minutes on the first side, or until the meat is brown. Turn the meat and cook for 3 minutes on the second side. Pour ½ cup of the wine into each of the skillets. Stir the meat back and forth so that it is completely coated with the wine. After a few seconds, transfer all of the cooked beef to an ovenproof serving dish. Keep the beef warm in the oven.

Combine all of the sauce and drippings in one skillet. Add the remaining wine and the mushrooms. Turn the heat to high and stir for a few minutes until the sauce thickens. Pour the mushroom sauce over the meat. Serve with the fettuccine, sprinkled with the grated cheese.

Yield: 4 servings.

Variation

To prepare Pépère's Veal Scallopini, substitute 1 pound of veal cutlets cut ⅜ inch thick for the round steak.

Grillades and Grits

One of New Orleans' most typical dishes is Grillades. It is often served for Sunday brunch or a midnight supper after a dance.

1½   teaspoons vegetable oil
 2   pounds top round steak, fat removed and cut ⅜ inch
      thick (Boneless beef rump can also be used.)
 2   large onions, coarsely chopped
 3   celery stalks, coarsely chopped
 2   garlic cloves, minced
 ½   teaspoon salt
 1   teaspoon ground black pepper
 2   tablespoons Kitchen Bouquet
 1   teaspoon dried thyme
1½   teaspoons chopped fresh parsley leaves
 3   teaspoons tomato paste (optional)
 3   to 4 cups water
 1   recipe hot Baked Grits (page 79)

Heat the oil in a large heavy pot over medium heat. Sauté the meat in the hot oil to sear it on both sides. Remove the meat to a dish when it is seared. Remove the pot from the heat.

Put the onions, celery, and garlic in the container of a blender. Process on medium speed until puréed. Pour the mixture into the pot in which the meat was seared and cook over medium heat for 5 minutes. Stir in the salt, pepper, Kitchen Bouquet, thyme, parsley, and tomato paste, if used. Return the meat to the pot and add the water. (Add more water, if necessary, to keep the meat covered by 1 inch.)

Bring to a simmer and cook, covered, over low heat for 1 to 1½ hours. (Beef rump will take 3 to 4½ hours to cook.) Add more hot water if the gravy becomes too thick. When cooked, the meat should be tender enough to cut with a fork. Taste for seasoning, and add salt and pepper, if necessary.

Serve the Grillades with the hot Baked Grits on the side. Spoon the gravy over both the Grillades and grits.
    Yield: 4 servings.

Williana's Pot Roast

4	tablespoons shortening
1½	pounds boneless beef chuck or bottom round, fat removed and the meat cut into 1- by 2- by 3-inch pieces
¼	cup unbleached white flour
1	large onion, cut into slices and the slices separated into rings
2	beef bouillon cubes
3¾	to 4 cups hot water
1	garlic clove, minced
½	teaspoon dried rosemary
½	teaspoon dried thyme
½	teaspoon salt
½	teaspoon ground black pepper
½	cup halved fresh mushrooms
4	large carrots, peeled and cut into 3-inch-long pieces
3	large potatoes, scrubbed, peeled, and cut into quarters
½	pound wide noodles, cooked *al dente,* following the package directions (optional)

Melt the shortening over medium heat in a very large heavy skillet or in a 3-quart saucepan. Add the meat and brown it quickly on all sides. Remove the meat to a plate as it browns. Add the flour to the fat remaining in the skillet and stir with a wooden spoon over medium heat until the mixture turns light brown. Add the onion to the skillet and sauté until it is tender.

Dissolve the bouillon cubes in ¾ cup of the hot water and add the mixture to the skillet. Stir the garlic, rosemary, thyme, salt, and pepper into the skillet, and return the meat to the skillet. Add the mushrooms, carrots, potatoes, and enough of the remaining water to cover the ingredients. Cover tightly and simmer over low heat for at least 3 hours, or until the meat is very tender. Add more water, if necessary, to keep the meat covered.

Serve hot, accompanied by the noodles, if desired.

Yield: 6 servings.

Puddin's Spaghetti Sauce

Meatballs

3	slices whole wheat bread
½	cup milk
1½	pounds lean ground beef
1½	pounds lean ground pork
6	eggs
½	teaspoon salt
½	teaspoon ground black pepper
1	medium-sized onion, minced
1	garlic clove, minced
1	tablespoon dried oregano
⅓	cup chopped fresh parsley leaves
⅓	cup unseasoned dry bread crumbs
½	cup freshly grated Romano cheese
2	tablespoons dry red wine
1	tablespoon Tabasco sauce

Sauce

2	pounds Italian sweet or hot sausage links
4	large loin pork chops
6	28-ounce cans whole Italian peeled tomatoes
3	6-ounce cans Italian tomato paste
2¼	cups water
1	15-ounce can tomato sauce
½	teaspoon salt
½	teaspoon ground black pepper
1	teaspoon dried oregano
1	garlic clove, minced
1	16-ounce can pitted black olives, drained and halved (optional)

Preheat the oven to 450 degrees.

To prepare the meatballs, put the bread and milk into a large bowl. Let soak for a few minutes; then mash the bread with a fork. Add the remaining ingredients and mix thoroughly, using your hand. Scoop up about 3 to 4 tablespoons of the meat mixture and mold it into a ball. Place the meatball on an ungreased jelly roll pan. You should be able to make 18 to 20 meatballs. Bake in the oven for 10 to 15 minutes. Then broil the meatballs for 7 to 9 minutes, or until the tops are brown. Set aside until needed. Reserve the drippings in the pan. Do not turn off the oven.

To prepare the sauce, put the sausage links in a baking pan and bake in the 450-degree oven for 7 to 10 minutes, or until they are light brown. Drain the fat from the pan and discard it. Remove the sausages from the pan and set them aside until needed. Put the pork chops in the same baking pan and broil them for 5 to 10 minutes, or until they are golden brown on both sides. Remove and discard any excess fat from the pork chops and set them aside.

Combine all of the ingredients for the sauce, except the pitted black olives, in a large pot. Mix well. Add the pork chops, sausage links, meatballs, and meatball drippings. Bring the sauce to a boil over medium heat. Lower the heat and simmer the sauce, partially covered, for 5 hours. Do not stir. If the sauce gets too thick, stir in a little water.

Remove the sauce from the heat and add the olives, if used. Let the sauce cool; then scoop the excess oil from the top of the sauce. The sauce can be stored in covered containers in the refrigerator for a few days or frozen.

To serve, reheat the sauce and serve it over cooked spaghetti with grated Romano cheese on top.

Yield: 12 servings.

Meat Loaf

Leftover meat loaf is great in sandwiches.

2   pounds lean ground beef
1   medium-sized onion, minced
1   teaspoon salt
1   teaspoon ground black pepper
2   garlic cloves, minced
2   eggs, slightly beaten
½   cup unseasoned dry bread crumbs
¾   cup milk
1   teaspoon Worcestershire sauce

Preheat the oven to 400 degrees.

Combine all the ingredients in a large mixing bowl. Mix by hand or with a large spoon for a few minutes, or until the mixture is a little stiff and thoroughly blended. Transfer the mixture to a loaf pan.

Bake, uncovered, for 1 hour, or until the center of the loaf is brown, not pink.

Drain off the grease and remove the meat loaf from the pan. Slice and serve hot or at room temperature.

Yield: 4 servings.

Baked Ham

1   7- to 8-pound smoked ham
30   to 40 whole cloves
½   cup dark brown sugar
½   teaspoon dry mustard
3   tablespoons apple cider vinegar

Preheat the oven to 350 degrees.

Place the ham in a large roasting pan. Bake, uncovered, for 45 minutes. Remove the ham from the oven and let it cool; then remove the skin and completely score the top and sides of the ham, making a 1½-inch diamond pattern all over. Insert the cloves at the points of the diamonds.

Mix the brown sugar, mustard, and vinegar together in a small bowl. Return the ham to the roasting pan and pour the glaze over the ham. Bake the ham in the 350-degree oven for 15 to 20 minutes, basting it frequently with the pan juices. Remove the ham from the oven and remove the cloves from the ham. Serve the ham warm or cold.

Yield: 8 servings.

Breaded Pork Chops

4	1-inch-thick large loin pork chops
¼	teaspoon salt
¼	teaspoon ground black pepper
¼	cup unbleached white flour
¼	cup unseasoned dry bread crumbs
2	tablespoons shortening

Trim the excess fat from the chops; then wash the chops and dry them on paper towels.

Combine the salt, pepper, flour, and bread crumbs in a plastic bag. Drop the chops into the mixture, one at a time, and toss to coat the chops completely.

Heat 1 tablespoon of the shortening in each of two 9-inch skillets over medium heat. Fry two chops in each skillet for 5 to 10 minutes on each side, or until they are tender and cooked through. Serve immediately.

Yield: 4 servings.

Variation

To prepare Breaded Veal Chops, substitute four 1-inch-thick veal chops for the pork chops.

Glazed Pork Chops

1 teaspoon salt
1 teaspoon ground black pepper
4 1-inch-thick loin pork chops
½ cup dark brown sugar
½ cup canned tomato sauce
¼ cup apple cider vinegar
¼ cup water

Mix the salt and pepper in a small bowl. Generously rub the mixture on both sides of each chop.

Heat two large skillets over medium heat. When the skillets are hot, turn the heat very low. Place the chops in the skillets.

Cook the chops for 2 minutes. Turn them over and sprinkle 1 tablespoon of the brown sugar on top of each chop. Cook for 2 minutes longer.

Turn the chops and sprinkle the remaining brown sugar over them. Cook for 1 more minute. Turn the chops again. The sugar should be caramelized.

Pour 1 tablespoon of the tomato sauce and 1 teaspoon of the vinegar on each chop. Turn the chops and pour the remaining tomato sauce and vinegar on top of them.

Simmer, uncovered, over low heat for 20 to 25 minutes, turning the chops every 5 minutes. Occasionally spoon some sauce from the skillet over the chops. If necessary, add a little water to keep the chops from sticking to the skillet. The chops should be glazed when they are done. Spoon the remaining glaze from the skillet over the chops and serve hot.

Yield: 4 servings.

Barbecued Ribs

Barbecue Sauce

¼	cup apple cider vinegar
½	cup water
2	tablespoons sugar
1	tablespoon prepared mustard
1½	teaspoons salt
½	teaspoon ground black pepper
¼	teaspoon cayenne pepper
1	teaspoon fresh lemon juice
1	medium-sized onion, finely chopped
¼	cup butter or margarine
½	cup canned tomato sauce
2	tablespoons Worcestershire sauce

2½	pounds (slab) pork spareribs or beef chuck flat ribs

Combine the sauce ingredients in a saucepan. Bring to a boil; then lower the heat and simmer, uncovered, for 20 minutes. Set aside. The sauce can be made in advance and poured into a jar and stored for up to two weeks in the refrigerator.

Preheat the oven to 350 degrees.

Place the ribs in a large baking pan. Bake, uncovered, for 20 minutes. Remove from the oven, turn the ribs, and baste thoroughly with the sauce. Cook for 20 more minutes. Turn the ribs and baste thoroughly with the sauce. Repeat turning and basting every 20 minutes. Bake the ribs for a total of 2½ hours, or until they are glazed on the outside and juicy inside.

To serve, heat the remaining sauce in a saucepan. Place the hot ribs on a serving platter. Pour the sauce over them and serve.

Yield: 2 servings.

Note: If the ribs are cut into individual pieces, reduce the baking time to a total of 1½ to 2 hours.

Roast Leg of Lamb

2	garlic cloves, minced
1⅛	teaspoons ground black pepper
1⅛	teaspoons salt
1	5½-pound leg of lamb at room temperature
¾	cup water

Preheat the oven to 350 degrees.

In a small bowl, combine the garlic with 1 teaspoon of the pepper and 1 teaspoon of the salt.

Use a sharp knife to make seven slits (½ inch wide and ½ inch deep) in the lamb. Fill the slits with the seasoning mixture. Rub any remaining mixture over the lamb. Place the lamb skin side up in a roasting pan. Roast, uncovered, for 2 to 2½ hours.

Remove the lamb from the oven and transfer it to a serving platter; cover with foil and keep warm. Pour the pan juices into a cup and let them stand for about 10 minutes, or until the fat rises to the top. Skim off and discard the fat. Pour the remaining pan juices back into the roasting pan. Add the water and put the roasting pan over very low heat. Use a wooden spoon to scrape up any browned-on bits in the pan. Season the gravy with the remaining salt and pepper.

Yield: 6 servings.

POULTRY

The subtropical climate of New Orleans is conducive to picnics in the parks year round. Whether in Audubon Park, once a sugar cane plantation and site of the 1884 Cotton Centennial Exposition; in City Park by the lagoons, amusement parks, and art museum; in Jackson Square surrounded by the Pontalba Apartments, St. Louis Cathedral, and the Cabildo and Presbytère museums; on the levee by the Mississippi River; or on the breakwater by Lake Pontchartrain, a good barbecue or bowl of Fried Chicken is usually a part of every outdoor feast.

New Orleanians have even been known to have picnics in the old cemeteries around the city. Since New Orleans is three feet below sea level, most of the cemeteries are above ground and are called "cities of the dead." Many of the tombs look like small houses; they are etched with family history and symbols. After a visit, people often rest in the shade of a large magnolia or oak tree and have a quiet, peaceful lunch in communion with the spirits.

Barbecued Chicken

Outdoor picnics with barbecued chicken are all-time favorites in the warm South.

1	10-ounce bottle Worcestershire sauce
1	10-ounce can beer
½	cup butter or margarine
3	1½-pound chickens, split in half
1	teaspoon salt
1	teaspoon ground black pepper

First prepare the grill for cooking the chicken: Line a 20- or 22-inch grill with heavy duty aluminum foil. Pour enough coals into the grill to cover the bottom completely. Push the coals toward the center. Light the coals 40 to 60 minutes before you are ready to start cooking. The coals are ready when they are very hot and coated with gray ash, and when no flames appear. When you are ready to cook, spread the coals out to cover the bottom of the grill. Place the rack about 6 inches above the hot coals. Also place a glass of water near the grill to use to douse the flames if they spurt up during cooking.

While the coals are heating, prepare the sauce by combining the Worcestershire sauce, beer, and butter in a saucepan. Cook for a few minutes over medium heat. Then remove the sauce from the heat and set it aside until needed.

Sprinkle the chicken halves on both sides with the salt and pepper and put them in a large roasting pan. Set the chickens aside until needed.

When the coals are ready, place the chicken on the uncovered grill, bony side down. Baste the chicken with the sauce and cook for 20 minutes, turning once. Baste again and cook for 20 to 30 minutes, basting frequently, until the meat is white, not pink, when it is pierced with a fork. Serve the chicken with any remaining sauce, reheated, on the side.

Yield: 6 servings.

Note: If you wish, you can bake the chicken in a 350-degree oven before you put it over the hot coals. Baste the chicken twice with the sauce and bake it for 30 minutes. Then transfer the chicken, bony side down, to the grill and cook, turning every 15 minutes, for 45 minutes, basting frequently with the sauce.

Fried Chicken

1	3-pound chicken, cut into 8 serving pieces
1	teaspoon salt
1	teaspoon ground black pepper
¼	cup unbleached white flour
¼	cup unseasoned dry bread crumbs
4	cups shortening

Sprinkle the chicken on all sides with the salt and pepper.

Combine the flour and bread crumbs in a plastic bag. Drop the chicken into the mixture, a few pieces at a time, and toss to coat the chicken completely. Put the coated chicken pieces on a platter.

Heat 2 cups of shortening in each of two large skillets over medium-high heat. The shortening should be smoking slightly when it is ready.

Put the chicken pieces into the skillets. Cook for about 15 minutes over medium-high heat, turning the pieces three or four times. Drain the chicken on paper towels or a brown paper bag. Serve warm or cold.

Yield: 4 servings.

Chicken Fricassée

2	tablespoons shortening
1	tablespoon unbleached white flour
1	small onion, minced
2	2½-pound chickens, each cut into 8 pieces
6	cups water
1	teaspoon salt
1	teaspoon ground black pepper
3	tablespoons Kitchen Bouquet
2	garlic cloves, minced
1	bay leaf
1	teaspoon cornstarch dissolved in 1 teaspoon cold water
6	cups hot Steamed Rice (page 76)

Melt the shortening in a large deep pot. Add the flour and stir until the mixture is smooth. Stir in the onions and cook until they are soft but not brown.

Add the chicken pieces to the pot, placing the bony pieces on the bottom. Cover the chicken with the water. Then add the salt, pepper, Kitchen Bouquet, garlic, and bay leaf to the pot. Bring to a boil, lower the heat, and simmer, uncovered, for 1 to 1½ hours. Stir gently after 15 minutes. When cooked, the chicken should be very tender, with the meat almost falling off the bones.

Stir the cornstarch mixture into the pot and simmer gently for 5 minutes longer. The gravy should be dark brown and thin.

Let the fricassée cool and then refrigerate it for a few hours so that the grease rises to the top. Skim the grease from the top and reheat the fricassée. Serve with the hot rice on the side. Spoon the hot gravy over the rice.

Yield: 8 servings.

Chicken Véronique

⅓ cup unbleached white flour
½ teaspoon salt
½ teaspoon ground black pepper
4 chicken breast halves, skinned
1 tablespoon butter or margarine
1 tablespoon vegetable oil
¾ cup Hollandaise Sauce (page 108)
3 tablespoons dry vermouth
2 tablespoons sour cream
15 seedless green grapes, washed and cut in half

Preheat the oven to 325 degrees.

Mix the flour, salt, and pepper together on a sheet of wax paper. Dredge the chicken pieces in the flour.

Heat the butter and oil in a skillet. Brown the chicken on both sides over medium heat. Transfer the browned chicken to a small baking dish and bake in the oven for 45 minutes.

Just before you are ready to serve, prepare the Hollandaise Sauce. Stir the vermouth and sour cream into the sauce and pour the hot sauce over the chicken breasts. Sprinkle the grapes on top and serve immediately.

Yield: 4 servings.

Roast Turkey with Gravy

If you wish, you can stuff this turkey with Corn Bread–Oyster Dressing (page 114-15). Be sure to include Charlotte's Cranberry Sauce (page 113) in the menu.

1	12-pound ready-to-cook turkey
3	teaspoons salt
3	teaspoons ground black pepper

Gravy

	Turkey giblets (heart, liver, gizzard, and neck)
¼	teaspoon salt
¼	teaspoon ground black pepper
4	cups water

Preheat the oven to 350 degrees.

Rinse the turkey, inside and out, under cool running water. Pat dry with paper towels.

Mix the salt and pepper together and sprinkle the turkey, inside and out, with the mixture. Place the turkey, breast side up, in a roasting pan, tucking the wings under the turkey. Lay a piece of aluminum foil over the turkey and roast for about 25 minutes to the pound, or 5 to 6 hours. Check the turkey every hour, basting it with the pan juices when you do. When the turkey is cooked, the legs will move up and down easily.

To prepare the gravy, cut the giblets (except the neck) in half and put them all in a pot with the salt, pepper, and water. Cover and bring to a boil. Lower the heat and simmer for about 1 hour, or until they are tender. Strain the broth and discard the giblets.

When the turkey is cooked, remove it from the roasting pan and transfer it to a platter.

Pour the strained turkey broth into a saucepan and scrape into the saucepan all of the drippings from the roasting pan. Simmer, uncovered, for 5 minutes. Taste for seasoning, adding more salt and pepper, if necessary.

Yield: 10 servings.

Grand-Mère's Roasted Quail

This is a full meal in itself. It is delicious and needs only a salad to make it complete. In France, a *pintadeau* (young guinea hen) is used instead of quail.

4	strips lard, about 1 ounce each, cut ⅛ to ¼ inch thick
2	quail or Cornish game hens
6	tablespoons butter or margarine
18	shallots, peeled but left whole
4½	cups water
2¼	teaspoons salt
2	beef bouillon cubes
6	ounces lean slab bacon, cut into 1- by 2- by 1-inch chunks
1¼	teaspoons ground black pepper
½	cup dry white wine
1	medium-sized carrot, peeled and cut into chunks
1	medium-sized onion, cut into quarters
1	scallion, chopped
1	pound small white potatoes
1	tablespoon vegetable oil
1	pound large fresh mushrooms, washed and dried
¼	teaspoon sugar
2	tablespoons Kitchen Bouquet
1	tablespoon Cognac
2	tablespoons fresh lemon juice
¼	cup chopped fresh parsley leaves

Wrap the strips of lard around the breasts of each bird, tying them in place with string that goes vertically and horizontally around the bird.

Heat 1 tablespoon of the butter in a large pot. Add the birds and brown them on all sides, grasping them by the legs to turn them.

Preheat the oven to 300 degrees.

Put the shallots into a medium-sized saucepan. Add 2 cups of the water and 1 teaspoon of the salt. Bring to a boil and cook for 20 minutes. Set the shallots aside.

Dissolve the beef bouillon cubes in 2 cups of the water in another pot. Add the slab bacon chunks. Bring to a boil, lower the heat, and simmer for 15 minutes. Drain and set the bacon cubes aside.

When the birds have finished browning, transfer them to a large baking dish. Sprinkle the birds with 1 teaspoon of the salt and 1 teaspoon of the pepper. Pour the wine and ½ cup of the water into the baking dish. Bake the birds, half covered, for 15 minutes.

Melt 2 tablespoons of the butter in a skillet. Add the carrot, onion, and scallion. Sauté until the vegetables are tender. Set aside for the gravy.

Peel the potatoes and cut them into 1½-inch ovals. Round the edges well so they will brown easily on all sides. Melt 1 tablespoon of the butter and the oil in a pie plate in the 300-degree oven. Then add the potatoes to the pie plate and sprinkle them with ¼ teaspoon of the salt and ¼ teaspoon of the pepper. Stir well to coat the potatoes with the butter. Bake them for 1 hour, or until they are tender when pierced with a fork. Shake the pan occasionally so the potatoes do not stick and can brown on all sides.

Remove the stems from the mushrooms, leaving the mushroom caps whole. Chop the stems. In a large skillet, melt 1 tablespoon of the butter over medium heat. Add the mushroom caps and stems and sauté for 3 to 4 minutes, or until the mushrooms are tender. Remove the mushrooms and set them aside in a small baking dish.

Add the cooked bacon chunks to the same skillet in which the mushrooms were cooked. Cook until they are well done and crisp. Drain the bacon on paper towels or a brown paper bag and transfer it to a small baking dish.

When the potatoes and quail are cooked, remove them from the oven. Discard the butter from the potatoes and set the potatoes and quail aside. Raise the oven temperature to 450 degrees.

Heat 1 tablespoon of the butter and the sugar in a large skillet. Add the shallots and sauté them until they are light brown. Drain well and add the shallots to the potatoes.

Transfer the birds from the baking dish to a platter. Pour the cooking liquids from the baking dish through a strainer into a small saucepan. Mash the carrot, onion, and scallion mixture through the strainer into the saucepan. Add ¼ cup water, Kitchen Bouquet, Cognac, and lemon juice to the saucepan. Simmer for 5 minutes and let cool for 30 minutes. Then scoop off any fat that has risen to the top of the gravy.

Remove the string and lard from the birds. Cut the birds in half and put the halves into a roasting pan. Heat the reserved potatoes and shallots, bacon, mushrooms, and birds in the 450-degree oven for 10 minutes. Heat the gravy on top of the stove.

To serve, center the quail halves on a large serving platter. Place the potatoes, shallots, bacon, and mushrooms decoratively around the edge of the platter. Pour half of the hot gravy over the completed dish and sprinkle the parsley on top. Serve immediately, passing the remaining hot gravy in a sauceboat.

Yield: 4 servings.

FISH & SHELLFISH

New Orleans is one of the largest port cities in the world. Its docks bustle with international trade. In the past, sacks of oysters and fresh fish were carried from its docks into the fish markets. Now they are transported by truck.

Nearby lakes, rivers, and the Gulf of Mexico flourish with Spanish mackerel, red fish, flounder, sheepshead, speckled trout, catfish, frog, turtle, oyster, shrimp, crab, and crawfish. Back home in the kitchen, these indigenous delicacies are transformed into Courtbouillon, Trout Marguéry, or Shrimp Creole.

Red Fish Courtbouillon

If red fish or red snapper are not available, use a local fish that is thick and firm and not oily. It should also be able to be cooked for a long period of time. Courtbouillon (pronounced COO-be-yon) literally means "a short soup."

Serve the fish with Mashed Potatoes (page 90), spooning the sauce from the pan over the potatoes and fish in each serving.

1	tablespoon vegetable oil
1	medium-sized onion, minced
1	16-ounce can whole tomatoes
1	tablespoon tomato paste
½	teaspoon salt
¾	teaspoon ground black pepper
1	4-pound red fish, cleaned and with head removed

Heat the oil over medium heat in a large saucepan. Add the onions and sauté until they are tender. Add the tomatoes, tomato paste, salt, and pepper. Simmer, uncovered, for about 20 minutes, or until the sauce has thickened. Push the sauce through a sieve into a bowl, pressing the solid ingredients to extract all of the moisture.

Preheat the oven to 350 degrees.

Place the fish in a large roasting pan. Pour the sauce over the fish to cover it completely. Bake the fish for about 1 hour, basting it occasionally with the sauce. The fish is done when the flesh looks dry when it is separated by a fork. Serve immediately.

Yield: 4 servings.

Note: The fish can also be cut into 1½-inch steaks. Bake the steaks for about 45 minutes.

Fried Trout

        3   eggs
       ½   cup unseasoned dry bread crumbs
        1   teaspoon dried oregano
       ¼   teaspoon salt
       ¼   teaspoon ground black pepper
       ½   cup sliced almonds (optional)
       ½   cup butter or margarine
        1   garlic clove, minced
        4   pounds fresh trout fillets
        1   tablespoon minced fresh parsley leaves
        1   lemon, sliced

Beat the eggs in a shallow bowl. Combine the bread crumbs, oregano, salt, pepper, and almonds, if used, on a large piece of wax paper.

Melt ¼ cup of the butter in each of two large skillets. Add half the garlic to each skillet and sauté until the garlic is just light brown.

Dip each piece of fish first into the beaten egg and then into the bread crumb mix. Then repeat the procedure with the egg and bread crumbs again. Place the coated fillets in the skillets. Cook, until brown, over low-to-medium heat, about 5 minutes. Turn the fillets and cook on the other side for about 5 minutes. Test the fish for doneness by separating the flesh with a fork. If it looks dry, it is done. Serve immediately, sprinkling the parsley on top and garnishing each serving with the lemon slices.

Yield: 4 servings.

Trout Marguéry

3	tablespoons olive oil
4	pounds fresh trout fillets, or one 8-pound whole trout, cleaned, skinned, and boned
½	cup water
¼	teaspoon salt
¼	teaspoon ground black pepper
1	recipe Hollandaise Sauce (page 108)
12	large fresh shrimp, peeled, deveined, and minced
1	4-ounce can mushrooms, drained and minced

Preheat the oven to 400 degrees.

Spread the olive oil over the bottom and sides of a large oven-proof baking dish. Lay the fillets in the dish. Pour the water into the dish and sprinkle the fish with salt and pepper.

Bake, uncovered, for 15 minutes. Remove the fish from the oven and pour ⅓ cup of the cooking juices from the dish into a small saucepan. Turn off the oven heat and return the fish to the oven to keep it warm.

While the fish is cooking, prepare the Hollandaise Sauce.

Add the chopped shrimp and mushrooms to the cooking juices and cook over medium heat for about 5 minutes, or until most of the liquid has evaporated.

Stir the mushroom and shrimp mixture into the Hollandaise Sauce. Remove the fish from the oven and pour the sauce over it. Serve immediately.

Yield: 6 servings.

Fried Soft-Shell Crabs with Almonds

Topping

20	tablespoons butter or margarine
3	cups sliced almonds

Soft-Shell Crabs

12	soft-shell crabs
1	cup heavy cream
2	eggs, beaten
½	teaspoon salt
¼	teaspoon ground black pepper
½	to 1 cup unbleached white flour
4	cups vegetable oil
6	lemons, cut in half

To prepare the topping, melt the butter in a large skillet over low heat. Add the almonds and sauté, stirring, until they are golden brown, about 10 minutes. Set aside and keep warm.

To prepare the crabs, remove the fibrous lungs by lifting the sides of the top shell; then cut off the face. (Or you can ask your fishmonger to prepare the crabs for you.)

Combine the cream, eggs, salt, and pepper in a large mixing bowl. Spread the flour on a piece of wax paper.

Dredge the crabs in the flour and then dip them into the cream mixture. Then coat the crabs again with the flour.

Preheat the oven to 300 degrees.

Heat 2 cups of oil in each of two large skillets. Fry 2 to 3 crabs in each skillet over high heat until they are golden brown. Turn and fry on the other side for 5 to 10 minutes, or until golden brown. Drain on paper towels or a brown paper bag. Keep the cooked crabs warm in the oven.

To serve, reheat the almonds in the skillet for 3 minutes, stirring occasionally. Spoon ¼ cup of the almonds over each crab and pour any remaining butter in the skillet over the almonds. Garnish each serving with 2 lemon halves.

Yield: 6 servings.

Crab Meat and Artichoke Casserole

4	to 6 Steamed Artichokes (page 82), or one 14-ounce can artichoke hearts, drained and quartered
12	ounces fresh lump crab meat
1	tablespoon fresh lemon juice
2	tablespoons olive oil
4	thin slices whole wheat bread, toasted
½	cup Hollandaise Sauce (page 108) at room temperature

Let the steamed artichokes cool for 10 minutes. Then remove the leaves and discard the choke. Set the hearts aside and use the leaves for another dish.

Preheat the oven to 350 degrees.

Place the artichoke hearts in the bottom of a 1-quart casserole. Spread the crab meat on top of the artichoke hearts. Sprinkle the lemon juice and olive oil on top of the crab meat. Bake, uncovered, for 20 minutes.

Place the toasted bread on an ovenproof serving platter. Transfer 1 artichoke heart and its crab meat to each piece of toast. Bake for 7 minutes. Remove from the oven and pour 2 tablespoons of Hollandaise Sauce over each portion. Serve at once.

Yield: 4 to 6 servings.

Fried Oysters

24 fresh raw oysters, shucked
½ cup unbleached white flour
2½ cups vegetable oil
¼ teaspoon salt
¼ teaspoon ground black pepper
1 lemon, cut into quarters
½ cup ketchup
½ cup Tartare Sauce (page 111)

Preheat the oven to 300 degrees.

Pour the oysters into a colander and rinse under cool running water. Drain and pat the oysters dry with paper towels.

Pour the flour into a small plastic bag. Place 3 or 4 oysters in the bag of flour and shake until they are thoroughly coated. Put the oysters on a platter.

Heat the oil in a heavy 10-inch skillet over high heat. When the oil starts to smoke, lower the heat slightly. Place 12 oysters at a time into the hot oil.

Cook for 3 minutes and turn the oysters over. Cook for 3 minutes longer, or until they are golden brown. With a large slotted spoon, remove the oysters from the skillet and drain them thoroughly on paper towels or a brown paper bag. Repeat the process for the remaining oysters. Keep the cooked oysters covered and warm in the oven.

To serve, sprinkle the Fried Oysters lightly with salt and pepper. Serve immediately with the lemon, ketchup, and Tartare Sauce on the side.

Yield: 2 servings.

Variation

To make Fried Shrimp, substitute 24 peeled and deveined large fresh shrimp for the oysters. Cook the shrimp for only 2 minutes on each side.

Shrimp Creole

2 pounds large fresh shrimp, peeled and deveined
1 celery stalk, chopped
½ large onion, cut into quarters
2 garlic cloves, halved
1 tablespoon vegetable oil
1 15-ounce can tomato sauce
1 16-ounce can whole tomatoes
½ teaspoon salt
¼ teaspoon ground black pepper
1 tablespoon sugar
½ teaspoon cayenne pepper
2 cups water
4 cups hot cooked Steamed Rice (page 76)

Put the shrimp into a colander and rinse them under cool running water. Drain well.

Put the celery, onion, and garlic into the container of a blender and process until they are puréed.

Heat the oil in a large skillet over medium heat. Pour the puréed vegetables into the skillet and sauté for a few minutes. Turn the heat to low and add the tomato sauce, whole tomatoes, salt, pepper, sugar, cayenne pepper, and water to the skillet. Mix well. Simmer, uncovered, for about 35 to 40 minutes, or until the vegetables have cooked down and the sauce has thickened. Pour the sauce through a strainer, pressing the vegetables with the back of a spoon to extract all of the liquid. Return the sauce to the skillet. Add the shrimp and simmer for 5 minutes.

To serve, spoon the sauce and shrimp over portions of the hot rice.

Yield: 6 servings.

Creamed Tuna on Toast

In the days when Catholics could not eat meat on Fridays, we often had Creamed Tuna on Toast for Friday night dinners. If it was not Creamed Tuna, then it was Seafood Gumbo or Fried Fish. Although the "no meat" abstention no longer exists, Creamed Tuna is still a Friday night treat.

2   tablespoons butter or margarine
1   tablespoon unbleached white flour
½   cup milk
⅛   teaspoon salt
¼   teaspoon ground black pepper
1   6½-ounce can light chunk tuna in water, drained
2   slices whole wheat bread, toasted

Melt the butter in a saucepan over low heat. Add the flour and mix thoroughly. Add the milk and stir with a wooden spoon for 3 to 4 minutes, or until the sauce has thickened. The sauce should coat the spoon. Remove the sauce from the heat.

Add salt and pepper and stir well. Add the tuna and mix thoroughly.

To serve, place 1 slice of toast on each serving plate. Generously spoon ½ cup hot Creamed Tuna over each slice. Serve immediately.

Yield: 2 servings.

PASTA, RICE & GRITS

Creole cuisine, though rooted in the French, Spanish, African, and West Indian cuisines, has been influenced by other factors. The large Italian population in New Orleans has made Creole Italian cuisine very popular. The native Indian tribes, predominantly the Choctaw tribe, contributed grits to the Creole diet. Creole cooking has also greatly benefited from the mass production of rice in the prairie region of southwest Louisiana. New Orleanians love grits and rice the way most other people love potatoes.

Stuffed Manicotti

Tomato Sauce

2	tablespoons olive oil
2	tablespoons minced onion
2	garlic cloves, minced
1	pound fresh mushrooms, washed and minced
2	15-ounce cans tomato sauce
1	teaspoon dried oregano
1	teaspoon dried marjoram
1	teaspoon dried tarragon

Stuffing

2	pounds lean ground beef (Cook in a skillet until brown; then drain the grease.)
½	cup chopped scallions
¼	cup chopped fresh parsley leaves
4	slices whole wheat bread
⅓	cup water

Manicotti

4	quarts water
1	teaspoon salt
1	tablespoon vegetable oil
8	ounces manicotti shells
1	teaspoon vegetable oil

Topping

4	ounces fresh Parmesan cheese, grated
8	ounces fresh mozzarella cheese, very thinly sliced

To prepare the sauce, heat the olive oil in a medium-sized skillet. Add the onion, garlic, and mushrooms. Sauté over low heat for 10 minutes, or until tender. Stir occasionally. Pour into a 1-quart saucepan. Stir in the tomato sauce, oregano, marjoram, and tarragon. Simmer for 5 minutes, stirring occasionally. Set aside.

To prepare the stuffing, mix the cooked ground beef, scallions, and parsley together in a large bowl. Soak the bread in the water until it is soggy. Tear the bread into pieces and add it to the beef mixture. Mix thoroughly and set aside.

To cook the pasta, bring the water, salt, and oil to a boil in a

6-quart pot. Add the manicotti and lower the heat slightly. Cook for about 15 minutes, or until the pasta is *al dente*. Stir occasionally. Carefully drain the manicotti in a colander. Let cool for 5 minutes.

Preheat the oven to 350 degrees.

Grease two 12- by 7- by 2-inch baking dishes. Spread ¼ cup of the sauce in each dish so that the bottoms of the dishes are completely covered.

Stuff the manicotti with the beef mixture. Place the manicotti side by side in the baking dishes. Sprinkle half of the Parmesan cheese on top; then pour on half of the tomato sauce. Add the remaining Parmesan cheese and then the remaining sauce. Spread the mozzarella cheese slices on top. Bake for 25 to 30 minutes. Serve 2 hot stuffed manicotti shells per person.

Yield: 6 servings.

Baked Macaroni and Cheese

1	pound elbow macaroni
1	teaspoon vegetable oil
10	ounces sharp Cheddar cheese, grated
3	tablespoons butter or margarine
1½	teaspoons salt
1½	teaspoons ground black pepper
2	cups milk

Cook the elbow macaroni until it is *al dente,* following the package directions. Drain in a colander, rinse under cool running water, and drain well.

Preheat the oven to 350 degrees.

Use the oil to grease the bottom and sides of a 3-quart baking dish. Put half of the cooked macaroni into the dish. Sprinkle half of the grated cheese over the macaroni. Put the remaining macaroni into the dish and sprinkle it with the remaining cheese. Dot the butter over the top.

Combine the salt, pepper, and milk and pour the mixture over the macaroni and cheese in the baking dish. Bake for 40 to 50 minutes, or until the top is brown and the milk has been absorbed by the macaroni. Serve hot.

Yield: 12 servings.

Steamed Rice

8 cups water
½ teaspoon salt
1 cup long-grain rice

Bring 4 cups of the water and the salt to a boil in a 3-quart pot. Lower the heat to medium and add the rice. Stir and boil, uncovered, for 15 minutes. Drain the rice in a colander.

Rinse the pot out and add the remaining 4 cups of water. Bring the water to a low boil. Place the colander containing the rice over the pot and steam the rice over medium heat for 15 to 20 minutes, or until it is tender. Stir the rice every 5 minutes to keep it from drying out.

Rice prepared this way will be light and fluffy, not sticky. The cooked rice will keep in the refrigerator for days if stored in an airtight container.

To reheat, put the rice in a colander and place the colander in a 2-quart saucepan over 4 cups of water. Bring the water to a boil. Cover the rice loosely with a lid. Steam for 10 minutes, or until the rice is very hot.

Yield: 2⅔ cups rice; 4 servings.

Note: For recipes using more or less than 1 cup of uncooked rice, make the necessary adjustments in the quantity of rice. The amount of water used for both boiling and steaming and the salt can remain the same for quantities up to 3½ cups of uncooked rice. For larger quantities, add a little more water and salt. For recipes using half-cooked rice, follow the directions above for boiling. After the rice has boiled and been drained, it will be ready to use in such recipes.

Mushroom Rice

1   tablespoon vegetable oil
1   small onion, minced
3   celery stalks, minced
3   scallions, minced
½   cup water
1   pound fresh mushrooms, washed and dried
1   teaspoon butter or margarine
½   pound chicken livers, minced
6   cups hot Steamed Rice (see opposite)
2   tablespoons chopped fresh parsley leaves
1   teaspoon salt
1   teaspoon ground black pepper

Heat the oil in a large skillet. Add the onion, celery, and scallions. Sauté until the vegetables are tender. Add the water and mushrooms and cook for 2 to 3 minutes, or until the mushrooms are tender. Pour the vegetable mixture into a bowl and set it aside.

Melt the butter in the skillet. Add the chicken livers and sauté for about 5 minutes. Return the vegetable mixture to the skillet and add the hot rice and parsley. Mix thoroughly, seasoning with the salt and pepper. Serve hot.

Yield: 6 servings.

Jambalaya

Leftover Jambalaya can be used as a stuffing for sweet green peppers, tomatoes, or squash. For a tasty treat, use it to stuff a turkey.

1	teaspoon vegetable oil
1	medium-sized onion, minced
3	garlic cloves, minced
1	16-ounce can whole tomatoes, drained and chopped
1	tablespoon tomato paste
1	cup water
1	pound smoked sausage, cut into ½-inch cubes
½	teaspoon salt
1	teaspoon ground black pepper
2⅔	cups hot Steamed Rice (page 76)

Heat the oil over medium heat in a large skillet. Add the onion and garlic and sauté for 5 minutes, or until the vegetables are tender. Add the tomatoes, tomato paste, and water. Simmer over low heat, uncovered, for 20 to 25 minutes.

Add the sausage, salt, and pepper to the skillet. Cover and simmer for 15 minutes. Then add the hot rice and mix well. Cook for 5 minutes over medium heat, stirring occasionally. Serve hot.

Yield: 4 servings.

Variations

Any one of the following can be substituted for the smoked sausage: 1 pound peeled and deveined fresh shrimp (add during the last 5 minutes of cooking only); 1 pound diced lean pork; 1 pound diced ham; 1 pound diced chicken; 1 pound diced turkey; or 1 pound diced top round, sautéed in bacon drippings.

Boiled Grits

Southerners eat plenty of grits and rice. My Aunt Lulu recalls that as a child she had grits every morning as part of her breakfast, and rice was always served at dinner.

    4   cups water
    1   teaspoon salt
    1   cup quick yellow or white grits
    1   to 2 tablespoons butter or margarine (optional)

Bring the water and salt to a rapid boil in a 2-quart saucepan over medium heat. Slowly stir in the grits. Let the mixture return to a boil; then lower the heat and simmer, uncovered, for 10 to 12 minutes. Stir the grits occasionally to keep them from sticking to the bottom and sides of the pan. When done, the grits should be thick and not watery. Serve hot, with a dab of butter on top, if you wish.
    Yield: 4 servings.

Baked Grits

    1   recipe Boiled Grits (see above)
    ½   cup milk
    4   tablespoons butter or margarine
    ½   teaspoon vegetable oil

Preheat the oven to 350 degrees.
    Prepare the Boiled Grits. When they are cooked, add the milk and butter to the saucepan with the grits. Mix until the milk and butter are completely incorporated.
    Spread the oil over the bottom and sides of a 2-quart baking dish. Pour the grits mixture into the dish and bake for about 1 hour.
    Yield: 4 servings.

VEGETABLES

When we were children, my father occasionally took the family down to the French market for coffee and doughnuts. In the market, we strolled by the all-night fruit and vegetable stalls. Accompanied by the smell of hops from Jax Brewery and the echoes of foghorns from passing ships on the Mississippi, we immersed ourselves in the softly illuminated colors of fresh produce.

In each market stall, there were baskets of fresh mirlitons, okra, onions, peppers, eggplants, squash, cushaw, Creole tomatoes, artichokes, pecans, bananas, plantains, apples, pineapples, persimmons, satsumas, navel oranges, strawberries, blackberries, and mangos. Stalks of sugar cane, hanging strands of garlic, and truckloads of watermelon lined the sidewalks. We usually took home a bag of Creole tomatoes and a stalk of sugar cane to munch on in the car. The tomatoes were so red and ripe that with a few sprinkles of salt we could sink our teeth into them immediately and have a full meal. The following recipes such as Artichoke Casserole, Fried Bananas, Skillet Pole Beans, Red Beans and Rice, Baked Cushaw, and Stuffed Mirliton embellish the natural goodness of Louisiana produce.

Steamed Artichokes

1 teaspoon salt
7 quarts water
8 artichokes
1 pound butter or margarine, melted, or 2 cups
  Hollandaise Sauce (page 108), or 2 cups Vinaigrette
  (page 112)

In a large container or in the sink, dissolve the salt in 6 quarts of water. Soak the artichokes in the salted water for 10 minutes. Turn occasionally.

Rinse the artichokes under cool running water. Trim the stems so that the artichokes can stand upright.

Pour 1 quart water into a large deep pot. Place a steamer rack in the bottom of the pot. The water should be about ½ inch from the bottom of the rack.

Bring the water to a boil over medium heat. Place the artichokes on the rack. Cover the pot tightly. Steam the artichokes for 40 to 50 minutes. Check the water level after 15 minutes. If necessary, add 2 more cups of water.

When the leaves can be pulled off easily, the artichokes are done. Remove from the pot immediately; do not overcook. Drain the artichokes in a colander.

To serve the artichokes hot, give each person a hot artichoke and a small bowl of melted butter (about 2 ounces each) or Hollandaise Sauce in which to dip the leaves and heart. To serve cold, prepare the Vinaigrette. Serve 2 ounces per artichoke.

Yield: 8 servings.

Artichoke Casserole

  6   Steamed Artichokes (see opposite)
  4   tablespoons butter or margarine
  1   medium-sized onion, minced
10   ounces fresh mushrooms, washed and sliced
  1   cup Béchamel Sauce (page 110)
⅛   teaspoon Tabasco sauce
  2   teaspoons Worcestershire sauce
½   teaspoon salt
½   teaspoon ground black pepper
½   cup unseasoned dry bread crumbs

Remove the leaves from the artichokes and place them on a cutting board. Use a spoon to scrape most of the meat from the leaves. Put the meat in a bowl. Discard the leaves. Remove and discard the choke from the heart. Put the hearts in a 7- by 12- by 2-inch oiled casserole dish.

Preheat the oven to 350 degrees.

Melt the butter in a large skillet over medium heat. Add the onion and mushrooms and sauté for about 10 minutes, or until they are tender. Turn the heat to low and add the Béchamel Sauce. Simmer for 10 minutes, stirring occasionally. Remove from the heat. Add the artichoke scrapings, Tabasco and Worcestershire sauces, salt, and pepper.

Pour the mixture over the artichoke hearts and top with the bread crumbs. Bake for about 20 minutes, or until the top is brown. Serve hot.

Yield: 6 servings.

Variation

To make Artichoke-Oyster Casserole, add 2 dozen washed and drained shucked oysters to the Béchamel Sauce mixture before it is poured over the artichoke hearts in the casserole. If the oysters are added, the dish should be baked for a total of 40 minutes.

Stuffed Artichoke Hearts

4   Steamed Artichokes (page 82)
2   tablespoons butter or margarine
¼   teaspoon salt
¼   teaspoon ground black pepper
1   cup Hollandaise Sauce (page 108)

Remove the leaves from the cooled artichokes. Reserve the leaves and heart. Discard the choke.

Scrape the meat off of each leaf by placing the leaf on a cutting board. With the edge of a spoon close to the top of the leaf, press down and scrape off about 80 percent of the meat from the leaf. Reserve the meat in a bowl. Discard the leaves. There should be about 2 cups of meat.

Melt the butter in a large skillet. Add the artichoke meat, salt, and pepper. Stir continuously over medium heat for 5 minutes, or until thoroughly blended. The mixture should appear to be a little mashed. Let cool.

Preheat the oven to 350 degrees.

Place the artichoke hearts in a baking pan. Mold about ⅓ cup of the artichoke meat by hand into a hemisphere. Place the flat side of the handful facing down, on top of the heart. The top of the artichoke should now be curved. Repeat until all of the mixture is used.

Bake the artichokes for 15 minutes. Pour the room-temperature Hollandaise Sauce on top and serve immediately.

Yield: 4 servings.

Steamed Jerusalem Artichokes

Jerusalem artichokes, which are also known as sunchokes or *les topinambours,* are different from the globe-type artichokes.

They are tubers of the sunflower plant and have a crisp texture and nutty flavor.

My Aunt Esther adores her beloved *topinambours*. She serves them cold in salads, hot in a cream sauce, fried in a light batter, or as a stuffing for duck.

 1   pound Jerusalem artichokes
 2   tablespoons butter or margarine

Rinse and scrub the artichokes thoroughly under cool running water. Remove the strings from the roots.

Pour about 1 inch of water into the bottom of a large pot. Put a steamer basket into the pot and bring the water to a boil over medium heat.

Put the artichokes into the basket and cover the pot. Steam over medium heat for 15 minutes, or until the artichokes can be pierced with a fork. Do not overcook. Add more water to the pot to maintain the 1-inch level. Remove the artichokes when they are done.

If desired, let cool for 5 minutes and peel.

Melt the butter in a large saucepan. Add the artichokes and stir them well until they are coated with the butter. Serve hot.

Yield: 4 servings.

Jerusalem Artichokes with Cream Cheese Sauce

 1   pound Steamed Jerusalem Artichokes (see above)
 4   ounces cream cheese at room temperature
 ½   cup milk

Steam the artichokes as directed in the recipe.

To make the sauce, blend the cream cheese and milk with an electric mixer in a small bowl until smooth.

When the artichokes are cooked, remove them from the steamer basket and put them in a serving dish. Pour the room-temperature sauce over them and serve immediately.

Yield: 4 servings.

Fried Bananas

Fried bananas are often served as part of a dinner menu. At our house, a favorite birthday dinner is steak, rice, Fried Bananas, and Lettuce Fatigué (page 106).

  4   tablespoons butter or margarine
  6   firm medium-sized bananas, ripe but not too ripe
  1   tablespoon granulated sugar
  ¼   cup dark brown sugar
  1   tablespoon ground cinnamon
  1   tablespoon water

Melt 3 tablespoons of the butter in a large heavy skillet. Peel the bananas and slice them in half lengthwise. Make a single layer of the banana halves on the bottom of the skillet (see Note). Cook over medium heat until the bananas are brown on the bottom; then turn them over and brown them on the other side. Total cooking time should be 5 to 7 minutes. Use a spatula to carefully remove the bananas to a shallow serving dish. Cover the bananas and keep them warm.

When all the bananas have finished cooking, melt the remaining tablespoon of butter in the skillet. Add the sugars, cinnamon, and water. Cook, stirring, until the syrup thickens. Pour the syrup over the bananas and serve immediately.
Yield: 6 servings.

Note: All of the banana halves may not fit into the skillet at one time. In that case, do not crowd the skillet, but fry the bananas in two batches, adding more butter, if necessary.

Skillet Pole Beans

 2 pounds fresh pole beans, washed and ends and
     strings removed (String beans can be substituted for
     the pole beans.)
 1 6-ounce jar marinated artichoke hearts
 ½ cup olive oil
 1 tablespoon butter or margarine (For an authentic
     Creole touch, substitute 1 tablespoon bacon
     drippings for the butter.)
 1 garlic clove, chopped
 ¼ teaspoon salt
 ¼ teaspoon cayenne pepper
 ¼ teaspoon dried rosemary
 ¼ teaspoon dried basil
 1 tablespoon fresh lemon juice
 ½ cup freshly grated Romano cheese

Put the pole beans in a steamer basket over boiling water and steam for 5 minutes. Remove the beans and let them cool.

Remove the artichoke hearts from the marinade and set the marinade aside. Slice the artichoke hearts into strips.

Heat the olive oil and butter in a large skillet. Add the garlic and cook until it is light brown. Add the cooled beans, artichoke hearts, and marinade to the skillet. Cook over low heat for 4 minutes. Add the salt, cayenne pepper, rosemary, basil, and lemon juice to the skillet. Stir and cook for 2 minutes longer. Transfer the mixture to a large hot platter. Sprinkle with the grated cheese and serve immediately.

Yield: 4 servings.

HAIL TO THE RED BEAN!

In New Orleans, the red bean has reigned in rich popularity for many generations. The most sought-after dish for both natives and visitors is the fabulous Red Beans and Rice. In the Fertile Crescent City, the home of the red bean, it is as traditional as the baked bean is to Boston.

It is served in homes, especially on Monday nights; at dinner parties; and in many restaurants daily. One reason why Red Beans and Rice is a Monday night tradition goes back to the days when families had large midday Sunday dinners. There was usually a baked ham, and the ham bone was left over. Since Monday was usually laundry day, red beans seasoned with the ham bone could simmer on the stove for hours, unattended. Another reason for the tradition is that after a full weekend of parties, rich food, and plenty of drinks, a simple, solid, nutritious meal tastes good. On Mardi Gras Day, families in homes that line parade routes serve it to hungry revelers who drop by to watch the parade and to "pass a good time."

The red bean is even immortalized in silver. During the Carnival season, the "Silver Bean" is a treasured gift. A red bean has also been used as part of the Mardi Gras King Cake (pages 128–30).

Leftover red beans can be used in Red Bean Soup (page 24), or Red Bean Dip (page 2). For real adventure, try a cold red bean sandwich. Just spread a little mayonnaise on two pieces of bread and top with a few large spoonfuls of cold cooked red beans. I frequently took red bean sandwiches to school for lunch. Needless to say, I received some strange stares. But I got the last laugh: the sandwiches were delicious.

Red Beans and Rice

These beans taste better when they are made a day ahead and then reheated. They also freeze very well.

Do not remove the bay leaf before you serve the beans. Although it is not supposed to be eaten, the bay leaf brings good luck to the person who finds it in his or her portion.

1   pound dry red kidney beans (If available, the Camillia brand is best.)
8   cups water
1   large ham bone, or 2 ounces sliced ham
¼   teaspoon salt
¼   teaspoon ground black pepper
1   teaspoon Tabasco sauce
1   bay leaf
1   large onion, cut into quarters
1   celery stalk, cut into quarters
2   garlic cloves, cut into quarters
1   pound hot sausage, cut into 2-inch-long pieces (optional)
3   cups hot Steamed Rice (page 76)

Pick over the beans to remove any dirt and broken beans. Rinse the beans under cool running water and drain them. Put the beans in a large pot and cover them with water. (Use 5 to 6 cups of water.) Soak the beans overnight (see Note).

Drain and rinse the beans and put them into a large pot. Add the 8 cups of water, ham bone, salt, pepper, Tabasco sauce, and bay leaf.

Put the onion, celery, and garlic into the container of a blender. Process only until the vegetables are grated. Pour the vegetables into the beans and stir well. Bring to a boil; then lower the heat and simmer, covered, for 1 to 1½ hours. Stir the beans frequently during the first 20 minutes of cooking to keep them from sticking to the bottom of the pot.

After the beans have cooked for an hour, add the sausage, if used. If the beans are not tender after 1½ hours, add more boiling water and cook them until they are tender.

To serve, put ½-cup servings of the hot rice on individual serving plates. Pour ¾-cup servings of the beans and gravy over the rice.

Yield: 6 servings.

Note: If you cannot soak the beans overnight, you can cook them for 1 to 2 hours longer than the time given in the recipe, or until they are tender. Just make sure there is enough liquid in the pot and that the beans do not stick to the bottom of the pot.

Mashed Potatoes

5   large potatoes, scrubbed and cut in half lengthwise
½   cup milk
6   tablespoons butter or margarine
¼   teaspoon salt
½   teaspoon cayenne pepper

Put the potatoes in a steamer basket and steam them over boiling water for 20 to 25 minutes, or until they can be easily pierced with a fork. Cool for 5 minutes and then remove the skins.

Put the potatoes, milk, butter, salt, and cayenne pepper into a large bowl. Beat with an electric mixer on high speed until smooth and creamy. Reheat the potatoes in a saucepan over low heat, stirring frequently. If they become dry, stir in a little more milk. Serve hot.

Yield: 4 servings.

Potato Puffs

2   large potatoes, scrubbed and cut in half lengthwise
½   cup water
3   tablespoons butter or margarine
½   teaspoon salt
¼   teaspoon ground black pepper
½   cup unbleached white flour, sifted
1   egg, beaten
2   cups vegetable oil

Put the potatoes in a steamer basket and steam them over boiling water for 20 to 25 minutes, or until they can be easily pierced with a fork. Cool for 5 minutes and then remove the skins.

Put the potatoes into a bowl and mash them with a potato masher or fork until they are no longer lumpy. Set aside until needed.

Bring the water, butter, ¼ teaspoon of the salt, and the pepper to a boil in a small saucepan. When the butter has melted and the mixture is boiling, remove the pan from the heat. Add the flour all at once and beat quickly with a wooden spoon until the flour is completely incorporated. Add the egg and stir quickly to blend it in well. Return the pan to low heat and cook and stir constantly for 2 to 3 minutes. When the dough forms a ball and pulls away from the sides of the pan, remove it from the heat. Blend the mashed potatoes into the dough with a fork.

Preheat the oven to 200 degrees.

Form the puffs by shaping 1 tablespoon of the mixture into a ball. Lay the ball on a large platter. Continue forming balls with the remaining mixture.

Heat the oil in a large skillet over high heat. When the oil just begins to smoke, lower the heat to medium-high and drop 8 or 10 of the balls into the hot oil. The balls will puff up. Fry for 3 to 4 minutes, turning the balls occasionally with a slotted spoon. When the balls are golden brown, remove them from the skillet and drain them on paper towels or a brown paper bag on a large platter. The Potato Puffs can be kept warm in the oven.

Sprinkle the Potato Puffs with the remaining ¼ teaspoon of salt before serving.

Yield: approximately 32 puffs; 4 servings.

Bonne Mère's Sweet Potato Orange Cups

This is a family favorite for Thanksgiving and Christmas dinners.

4	large sweet potatoes, washed and cut in half lengthwise
2	teaspoons dark brown sugar
1	teaspoon ground cinnamon
1	teaspoon ground nutmeg
2	tablespoons butter or margarine
3	large navel oranges
⅓	cup orange juice (from the navel oranges)
⅓	cup chopped pecans
1	to 1½ cups water

Put the sweet potatoes in a steamer basket and steam them over boiling water for 20 to 30 minutes, or until they can be easily pierced with a fork. Cool for 5 minutes and then remove the skins.

Put the potatoes, brown sugar, cinnamon, nutmeg, and butter into a large bowl. Beat with an electric mixer on high speed until smooth and creamy. Set the mixture aside.

Wash the oranges and cut them in half horizontally. Gently squeeze and reserve the juice from the oranges, being careful not to break the orange skins. Strain the juice to remove the seeds. Use a spoon or your fingers to remove the pulp from the center of the orange halves. Set the hollowed-out orange halves aside.

Preheat the oven to 350 degrees.

Add the orange juice and pecans to the potatoes and mix well. Spoon the potato mixture into the orange cups and put the filled orange cups in a small baking dish. Place the baking dish in a larger baking pan and pour the water into the baking pan. Bake for 40 to 50 minutes, adding more water to the larger pan, if necessary.

Yield: 6 servings.

Baked Mashed Sweet Potatoes

  6 large sweet potatoes, washed and cut in half
       lengthwise
  8 tablespoons butter or margarine
  ⅓ cup dark brown sugar
  2 teaspoons ground cinnamon
  1 teaspoon ground nutmeg
  1 teaspoon pure vanilla extract
  1 teaspoon vegetable oil
 20 large marshmallows (optional)

Put the sweet potatoes in a steamer basket and steam them over boiling water for 20 to 30 minutes, or until they can be easily pierced with a fork. Cool for 5 minutes and then remove the skins.

Preheat the oven to 350 degrees.

Put the potatoes, butter, brown sugar, cinnamon, nutmeg, and vanilla into a large bowl. Beat with an electric mixer on high speed until smooth and creamy.

Use the oil to coat the bottom and sides of a baking dish. Spread the potato mixture in the baking dish. Place the marshmallows on top of the potato mixture, if using them, and push them about halfway down into the mixture. Bake for 20 minutes and serve hot.

Yield: 4 servings.

Creamed Spinach

---

3   10-ounce packages frozen chopped spinach
1   teaspoon salt
1   teaspoon ground black pepper
1   teaspoon butter or margarine
8   ounces cream cheese at room temperature, cubed
½   teaspoon vegetable oil

Put the spinach in a steamer basket and steam over boiling water for about 5 minutes, or until completely defrosted. Transfer the spinach to a colander and drain it thoroughly. (All of the excess water must be removed or the spinach will be too watery when it is baked.)

Preheat the oven to 350 degrees.

Put the drained spinach, salt, pepper, butter, and cream cheese into a large mixing bowl. Beat with an electric mixer on low speed for 1 to 2 minutes, or until thoroughly mixed.

Use the oil to coat the bottom and sides of a baking dish. Pour the spinach mixture into the dish and bake for 30 minutes. Serve hot.

Yield: 6 servings.

Spinach Casserole

2	10-ounce packages frozen chopped spinach
4	tablespoons butter or margarine
2	tablespoons unbleached white flour
2	tablespoons chopped onion
½	cup evaporated milk
½	teaspoon ground black pepper
⅛	teaspoon cayenne pepper
¾	teaspoon celery salt
2	garlic cloves, minced
1	teaspoon Worcestershire sauce
6	ounces jalapeño cheese, cubed
½	teaspoon vegetable oil
2	tablespoons unseasoned dry bread crumbs

Put the spinach in a steamer basket and steam over boiling water for about 5 minutes, or until completely defrosted. Transfer the spinach to a colander and let it drain thoroughly. (All of the excess water must be removed or the spinach will be too watery when it is baked.)

Melt the butter in a medium-sized saucepan. Add the flour and stir with a wooden spoon until the mixture is blended and smooth. Add the onion and cook until it is soft. Add the evaporated milk, black pepper, cayenne pepper, celery salt, garlic, Worcestershire sauce, and cheese. Stir until the cheese has melted. Stir in the well-drained spinach.

Preheat the oven to 350 degrees.

Use the oil to coat the bottom and sides of a baking dish. Pour the spinach mixture into the baking dish and sprinkle the bread crumbs on top. Bake for 10 to 15 minutes, or until very hot. Serve immediately.

Yield: 6 servings.

Note: This dish can be made ahead and refrigerated for a day. It also freezes very well.

Baked Cushaw

Cushaw is a type of crookneck winter squash found in Louisiana. If it is not available, butternut squash can be substituted.

1	3- to 4-pound cushaw squash
⅓	cup dark brown sugar
12	tablespoons butter or margarine, melted
2	teaspoons ground cinnamon
2	teaspoons ground nutmeg
2	teaspoons pure vanilla extract
2	teaspoons vegetable oil

Wash the cushaw; then cut it into 4-inch cubes and remove the seeds. Put the squash pieces in a steamer basket and steam them over boiling water for 5 minutes, or until they are tender. Let cool and then peel the skin from the squash.

Preheat the oven to 350 degrees.

Combine the brown sugar, butter, cinnamon, nutmeg, and vanilla in a large bowl. Add the cushaw and mash well. Purée the squash mixture in small batches in the container of a blender on low speed for 1 or 2 minutes. Pour the purée into another bowl. When all the squash has been puréed, stir it until it is well combined.

Spread the oil over the bottom and sides of two 9-inch pie plates. Pour equal amounts of the purée into each of the pie plates and bake for 50 minutes, or until the tops are light brown. Serve hot.

Yield: 8 servings.

Baked Mirliton

This southern vine-grown delicacy is also known as a vegetable pear or chayote. If mirlitons (pronounced mur-li-TAHN) are not available, zucchini or yellow crookneck squash can be substituted.

6	large mirlitons, or 4½ pounds zucchini or yellow crookneck squash
¾	cup chopped cooked ham
½	teaspoon salt
½	teaspoon ground black pepper
1	garlic clove, minced
1	tablespoon butter or margarine
½	cup unseasoned dry bread crumbs

Wash the mirlitons and then put them into a steamer basket. Steam them over boiling water until they can be easily pierced with a fork. Let the squashes cool and then slice them in half. Remove the seeds and use a spoon to scrape out the flesh of each squash. Discard the skins and put the flesh in a bowl. Mash the flesh and set it aside until needed.

Preheat the oven to 350 degrees.

Combine the ham, salt, pepper, garlic, butter, and mashed squash in a skillet. Bring to a boil and simmer for 10 to 15 minutes. Pour the mixture into a shallow 9-inch baking dish. Sprinkle the bread crumbs over the top. Bake for 20 to 30 minutes, or until the top is brown. Serve hot. (This does not freeze.)

Yield: 4 servings.

Stuffed Mirliton

This can be served as either a main dish or a side dish.

 4 large mirlitons, or 3 pounds zucchini or large yellow
    crookneck squash
 3 tablespoons vegetable oil
 1 large onion, diced
 ½ cup chopped celery
 1 pound fresh shrimp, peeled, deveined, and chopped
 1 cup unseasoned dry bread crumbs
 1 teaspoon salt
 ½ teaspoon ground black pepper
 3 tablespoons butter or margarine

Clean and cut the mirlitons in half lengthwise. (If using the squash, trim and discard the ends.) Remove the seeds. Put into a steamer basket and steam over boiling water for about 5 minutes, or until tender. Do not overcook. Drain and cool. Scoop out the mirliton pulp and put the pulp in a large bowl. Reserve the mirliton shells for stuffing. Mash the pulp with a potato masher.

Heat the oil in a large skillet and sauté the onion and celery for about 5 minutes, or until they are tender. Add the shrimp, ½ cup of the bread crumbs, mirliton pulp, salt, and pepper. Mix thoroughly.

Preheat the oven to 350 degrees.

Stuff the shells with the mirliton mix and place on a jelly roll pan. Top each shell with the remaining bread crumbs. Place about 1 teaspoon of butter on top of each shell. Bake for 30 minutes, or until the tops are brown. Serve hot.

Yield: 8 servings.

SALADS

When the sultry New Orleans summer makes you feel like you are walking in an outdoor steam bath, a cool salad for lunch or dinner is like manna in the desert. Blest by the abundance of fresh Louisiana produce, there is a wide selection of ingredients for salad creations. I find the Crabmeat and Grapefruit Salad and the Rice and Artichoke Hearts Salad to be my favorites during the summer heat wave.

Soup Meat Salad

This is served as a main dish both in private homes and in restaurants. When Vegetable Soup (pages 22–23) is prepared, usually once a week, the meat used to make the soup stock is saved to become part of this salad for the following night.

2   cups chopped cooked beef at room temperature
3   hard-boiled eggs, peeled and chopped
3   celery stalks, chopped
½   cup Mayonnaise (page 111)
4   large ripe tomatoes
    Leaves from ½ head romaine lettuce

Combine the beef, eggs, celery, and Mayonnaise in a large mixing bowl.

Wash the tomatoes and cut off the tops. Use a small spoon to scoop out the seeds. Drain the tomatoes briefly; then fill the tomatoes with the meat mixture. Place the tomatoes on a lettuce-lined salad plate to serve.

Yield: 4 servings.

Crab Meat and Grapefruit Salad

1   pound fresh lump crab meat
2   grapefruit
¼   cup fresh lemon juice
⅔   cup vegetable oil
¼   teaspoon salt
¼   teaspoon ground black pepper
1   ¾-pound romaine lettuce

Put the crab meat in a medium-sized bowl. Make sure all the shells are removed. Cover and refrigerate.

With a knife, remove all the rind and outer pulp from the grapefruit. Slice the grapefruit into ⅛-inch-thick slices across the segments so that the slices look like wheels with spokes. Remove all the seeds and slice the wheels in half. Place the segments in a bowl, cover, and refrigerate.

Put the lemon juice, oil, salt, and pepper in a jar with a tight-fitting lid. Shake well.

To serve, break the lettuce into bite-sized pieces and place it in individual salad bowls. Place grapefruit slices on top and then spread the crab meat over all. Shake the dressing and pour it on top. Toss lightly and serve.

Yield: 4 servings.

Variation
One cup of Vinaigrette (page 112) can be substituted for the dressing above.

Caesar Salad

4	garlic cloves, minced
1	2-ounce can anchovy fillets, mashed with a fork
3	tablespoons Worcestershire sauce
¼	cup fresh lemon juice
½	teaspoon salt
½	teaspoon ground black pepper
⅔	cup vegetable oil
⅓	cup apple cider vinegar
2	teaspoons dry mustard
¼	teaspoon Tabasco sauce
1	celery stalk, minced
4	egg yolks, beaten
½	cup freshly grated Parmesan cheese
3	heads romaine lettuce, washed, dried, and broken into bite-sized pieces
1	cup Croutons (page 125)

Combine the garlic, anchovies, Worcestershire sauce, lemon juice, salt, pepper, oil, vinegar, mustard, Tabasco sauce, celery, egg yolks, and grated cheese in a 16-ounce jar. Shake well.

Put the lettuce and Croutons in a large wooden bowl. Toss to mix well. Shake the dressing and pour it over the lettuce and Croutons. Toss again and serve on chilled plates.

Yield: 12 servings.

Rice and Artichoke Hearts Salad

This salad is fabulous in the summer. It can be a light, cool meal in itself.

½ cup apple cider vinegar
½ cup vegetable oil
½ teaspoon dried thyme
¼ teaspoon Tabasco sauce
¼ teaspoon salt
¼ teaspoon ground black pepper
1 8½-ounce can petit pois peas, drained
1 8-ounce jar marinated artichoke hearts
⅓ cup chopped scallions
6 fresh cherry tomatoes, washed and cut in half
4 cups cooked Steamed Rice (page 76) at room
    temperature
½ pound romaine lettuce, washed and dried

Mix the vinegar, oil, thyme, Tabasco sauce, salt, pepper, peas, artichoke hearts, scallions, and tomatoes in a bowl. Toss gently, cover, and refrigerate.

Just before serving, add the cooled rice to the mixture and stir thoroughly. Arrange lettuce leaves on serving platter or on individual dishes. Place the mixture on top of the lettuce. Use about 1 cup of the mixture for each serving.

Yield: 6 servings.

Egg and Bacon Salad

6 hard-boiled eggs, peeled and finely chopped
½ pound lean sliced bacon, cooked crisp and drained on
    paper towels or a brown paper bag
1 1-pound head romaine lettuce, washed, dried, and
    broken into bite-sized pieces
¼ cup Vinegar and Oil Dressing (page 112)

Put the eggs in a large salad bowl. Crumble the drained bacon
over the eggs. Add the lettuce and toss. Sprinkle the dressing
over the salad ingredients and toss again. Serve immediately.
    Yield: 4 servings.

Grapefruit and Avocado Salad

1 ½-pound head Bibb lettuce
1 ½-pound head romaine lettuce
2 large pink grapefruit, peeled and sliced, with
    membranes and seeds removed
1 large ripe avocado, peeled and sliced
¼ to ⅓ cup Vinegar and Oil Dressing (page 112)

Wash and dry the lettuce carefully. Then tear it into bite-sized
pieces. Put the lettuce pieces in a large salad bowl. Add the
sliced grapefruit and avocado. Sprinkle the dressing over the
salad, toss, and serve.
    Yield: 4 servings.

Potato Salad

4 large potatoes, scrubbed and cut in half lengthwise
2 celery stalks, chopped
2 hard-boiled eggs, peeled and sliced
½ teaspoon salt
1 teaspoon ground black pepper
⅔ cup Mayonnaise (page 111)
   Leaves from ¼ head romaine lettuce, washed and
   dried

Put the potatoes in a steamer basket and steam them over boiling water for 20 minutes, or until they can be easily pierced with a fork. Cool the potatoes and then remove the skins. Cut the potatoes into ½-inch cubes. Add the celery, eggs, salt, and pepper and mix well. Add the Mayonnaise and mix again. Cover and refrigerate the salad for a few hours before serving. Serve on a bed of lettuce.
   Yield: 6 servings.

Coleslaw

2 medium-sized heads green cabbage, cored, washed,
   and dried
½ cup Mayonnaise (page 111)
⅓ cup vegetable oil
6 tablespoons apple cider vinegar
¼ teaspoon salt
¼ teaspoon ground black pepper
2 teaspoons poppy seeds (optional)
1 cup applesauce (optional)

Shred the cabbage and put it in a large mixing bowl.
   Combine the Mayonnaise, oil, vinegar, salt, and pepper in a jar with a tight-fitting lid. Shake until the dressing is thoroughly

combined. Pour the dressing over the cabbage and toss well. Add the poppy seeds and applesauce, if desired, and toss again. Cover the bowl and refrigerate the salad for 30 to 60 minutes before serving.

   Yield: 8 servings.

Carrot and Raisin Salad

   1   pound carrots, washed, peeled, and shredded
   ⅔   cup dark raisins
   ½   cup Mayonnaise (page 111)
   1   1-pound head romaine lettuce, washed, dried, and
        broken into bite-sized pieces
   ⅓   cup Vinegar and Oil Dressing (page 112), optional

Combine the carrots, raisins, and Mayonnaise in a bowl and mix together thoroughly.

   Make a bed of the lettuce in six individual salad bowls. Top the lettuce with about ½ cup of the carrot mixture. If desired, pour a few teaspoons of the dressing on top of the salad before serving.

   Yield: 6 servings.

Lettuce Fatigué

---

    1   garlic clove, peeled
    8   2-inch-thick slices stale French bread, including 1 end
        piece
   ¾   cup Vinegar and Oil Dressing (page 112)
    3   pounds iceberg lettuce, washed and dried

Season a large wooden salad bowl by placing the peeled garlic in the end piece of French bread and rubbing it thoroughly over the inside of the bowl.

Remove the garlic from the bread. Add the bread to the other pieces of bread. Mince the garlic and add it to the dressing.

Tear the lettuce into bite-sized pieces and put it into the salad bowl. Break the bread into bite-sized pieces and scatter them over the lettuce.

Thirty minutes before serving, shake the dressing and pour it over the salad. Toss thoroughly and refrigerate the salad for 30 minutes. The lettuce should be slightly limp and the bread slightly soggy when it is served.

Yield: 6 servings.

SAUCES & ACCOMPANIMENTS

New Orleans cooking is famous not only for its spicy tastes but for its emphasis on making a lot out of a little, for being eccentrically rich with a poor man's budget, for making an ordinary dish fantastic by adding a little extra of this or that ingredient. The special touch of a well-seasoned sauce can change a good dish into a spectacular one.

Hollandaise Sauce

Hollandaise Sauce is excellent on grilled meats, seafood, and vegetables. It should not be reheated, but, if necessary, it can be kept warm for a little while in the top of a double boiler over just-simmering water. (Note: Do not use a Teflon-coated saucepan to make this sauce.)

2   tablespoons fresh lemon juice
2   egg yolks at room temperature
8   ounces cold butter or margarine (Cut each stick in half.)

Put the lemon juice and egg yolks into a small saucepan. Use a wooden spoon to thoroughly combine the lemon juice with the egg yolks.

Put the saucepan over low heat. Pierce 1 half-stick of the butter with a fork. Slowly stir the egg-yolk mixture with the half-stick of butter until the butter has melted. Do not let the sauce boil or get too hot. Tilt the pan, if necessary, to control the heat. Continue stirring the butter into the sauce until all of it has been used. The sauce should thicken slowly. Make sure that you come into contact with the bottom and sides of the pan while you are stirring. It should take about 7 to 10 minutes for the sauce to reach the proper consistency. As soon as it has thickened, remove the sauce from the heat.

Yield: 1 cup; 4 servings.

Béarnaise Sauce

This sauce makes a good accompaniment for grilled meats, seafood, and vegetables. It should not be reheated, but, if necessary, it can be kept warm for a little while in the top of a double boiler over just-simmering water.

½   cup dry white wine
¼   cup tarragon vinegar
¼   cup minced shallots
½   teaspoon ground black pepper
1   recipe Hollandaise Sauce (see above)

Combine the wine, vinegar, shallots, and pepper in a large saucepan. Bring to a boil over medium heat and cook until the liquid has been reduced by half. Let cool completely.

Add the cooled wine mixture to the hot Hollandaise Sauce and cook and stir for 20 seconds.

Yield: 1¼ cups; 6 servings.

Choron Sauce

This sauce goes very well with grilled meats, seafood, and vegetables. It should not be reheated, but, if necessary, it can be kept warm for a little while in the top of a double boiler over just-simmering water.

4   tablespoons butter or margarine
3   tablespoons minced shallots
¼   cup canned tomato sauce
1   recipe Béarnaise Sauce (see above)

Melt the butter in a small skillet over medium heat. Add the shallots and sauté for a few minutes, or until the shallots are tender. Stir in the tomato sauce, lower the heat, and cook the sauce for 10 minutes. Remove the sauce from the heat and let it cool completely.

Add the cooled sauce to the hot Béarnaise Sauce and mix well. Serve immediately.

Yield: 1½ cups; 8 servings.

Béchamel Sauce

       2   tablespoons butter or margarine
       3   tablespoons unbleached white flour
       2   cups milk, heated
      ½   teaspoon salt
      ¼   teaspoon ground black pepper
      ¼   teaspoon ground nutmeg
      ½   teaspoon dried thyme

In a saucepan, melt the butter over low heat. Use a wooden spoon to stir in the flour completely. Add the warm milk slowly, stirring constantly. Season the mixture with salt, pepper, nutmeg, and thyme. Cook, stirring constantly with a wooden spoon, until the sauce is smooth and has begun to simmer. Cook for 2 to 4 minutes, or until the sauce thickens. If the sauce becomes too thick, add a little more hot milk.

Yield: 2 cups; 8 servings.

Cheese Sauce

This sauce is particularly good when poured over steamed cauliflower.

       1   recipe Béchamel Sauce (see above)
      ½   cup grated sharp Cheddar cheese

When the Béchamel Sauce has thickened, stir in the grated cheese until it has melted completely. Remove from the heat and serve at once.

Yield: 2½ cups; 8 servings.

Mayonnaise

The difference in taste and quality between homemade and store-bought mayonnaise will be apparent to you very quickly. This simple recipe can easily be doubled, if necessary. It will keep in the refrigerator in a tightly closed jar for a week to ten days.

2   tablespoons fresh lemon juice
1   teaspoon dry mustard
1   teaspoon salt
2   eggs at room temperature
1   cup vegetable oil

Put the lemon juice, mustard, salt, eggs, and ¼ cup of the oil in the container of a blender. Cover and blend on medium-high speed for 20 seconds.

Remove the cover and, with the blender running, very slowly pour the rest of the oil into the center of the mixture. The sauce should thicken gradually. When all of the oil has been added, blend for an additional 30 to 60 seconds, or until the sauce is thick and firm. Pour the sauce into a jar and refrigerate.
Yield: 1½ cups.

Tartare Sauce

⅔   cup Mayonnaise (see above)
⅓   cup minced drained dill pickle

Combine the Mayonnaise and the dill pickle and mix well. Pour the sauce into a jar with a tight-fitting lid and store in the refrigerator.
Yield: 1 cup.

Vinaigrette

This is good as a salad dressing or as a dip for steamed artichoke leaves.

½ cup corn oil
½ cup olive oil
¼ cup fresh lemon juice
½ teaspoon salt
1 teaspoon dry mustard
3 shallots, minced
   Leaves from 3 sprigs fresh parsley, minced
⅛ teaspoon cayenne pepper

Put all the ingredients in the container of a blender and blend on medium speed for 1 minute.
Yield: 1¼ cups.

Vinegar and Oil Dressing

⅓ cup apple cider vinegar
⅔ cup vegetable oil
1 teaspoon salt
½ teaspoon ground black pepper
1 tablespoon Dijon mustard (optional)

Put all of the ingredients in a jar with a tight-fitting lid, cover, and shake well.
Yield: 1 cup.

Charlotte's Cranberry Sauce

Every time I make cranberry sauce, I am reminded of my brother's cub scout troop. One year, when my mother was den mother for the troop, she taught the boys how to make the sauce so they could give it to their mothers as a present. It was such a big success that she still makes it every year to give as presents and for our holiday feast tables.

    1   pound fresh cranberries, washed and drained
    2   oranges, washed, cut into quarters, and seeded
    1   lemon, washed, cut into quarters, and seeded
    2   cups sugar

Combine all the ingredients in a large mixing bowl.

Put a quarter of the mixture into the container of a blender and process on medium speed until chopped. Transfer the chopped mixture to a large bowl. Repeat the process until all the ingredients have been chopped.

Transfer the chopped mixture to jars with tight-fitting lids and store in the refrigerator. For best results, make the Cranberry Sauce at least 1 week before serving. It will keep in the refrigerator for up to 2 months.

Yield: 8 servings.

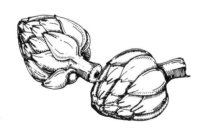

Corn Bread–Oyster Dressing

½	pound bulk hot sausage meat
5	celery stalks with leaves, minced
6	shallots, minced
1	large onion, minced
1	garlic clove, minced
¼	cup minced fresh parsley leaves
3	teaspoons dried rosemary
3	teaspoons crushed bay leaves
3	teaspoons dried thyme
3	teaspoons dried basil
3	teaspoons poultry seasoning
1½	cups milk
½	pound butter or margarine
2½	to 3 cups crumbled corn bread
1	cup unseasoned dry bread crumbs
1	egg, beaten
½	teaspoon salt
1	teaspoon ground black pepper
12	fresh oysters, shucked and minced
½	cup oyster liquor
1	teaspoon vegetable oil

Put the sausage meat into a large skillet and cook it over medium heat, stirring and breaking it up with a wooden spoon, until it is brown. Remove the sausage with a slotted spoon and set it aside.

Add the celery, shallots, onion, garlic, and parsley to the skillet and sauté in the sausage drippings until they are tender. Add the rosemary, bay leaves, thyme, basil, and poultry seasoning and mix well. Set the vegetables aside.

Put the milk and butter in a small saucepan. Heat over low heat until the butter has completely melted. Set aside to cool for 5 minutes.

In a large bowl, combine the crumbled corn bread, bread crumbs, sausage, and vegetables. Pour in the cooled milk and butter mixture and blend well. Then add the egg, salt, pepper, oysters, and oyster liquor. Mix well. If the stuffing looks too dry, add a little more milk.

The dressing can be used to stuff a turkey or it can be baked in a baking dish spread with the vegetable oil for 1 hour in a 350-degree oven. Remove any excess grease before serving.
Yield: 8 cups stuffing; 12 servings.

Variations
Any one of the following can be added to the stuffing mix along with the oysters: 1 pound fresh shrimp, peeled and deveined; ½ pound fresh lump crab meat; ½ cup pecans, chopped; ½ cup cooked rice; or ¼ cup caraway seeds.

Papou's Fig Preserves

As a child, I used to help my father pick ripe figs early every morning during the fig season. We would peel them and have them with cream for breakfast.

These fig preserves are delicious spread on hot biscuits (page 124) for breakfast. They make an equally good dessert when served with Cheddar cheese and crackers.

    8   cups whole fresh figs, stemmed and washed
    4   cups sugar
    ½   cup water
    ½   lemon, thinly sliced and seeded

Put all the ingredients in a heavy 3-quart pot. Bring to a boil, lower the heat, and simmer, uncovered, for 1 to 2 hours, or until the juice is reddish-brown and the consistency of a syrup. Stir occasionally while cooking.

Let the preserves cool and pour them into jars with tight-fitting lids. Store in the refrigerator.
Yield: 3 pints.

Tante Emma's Pear Preserves

Tante Emma lived on *Île Dernière*, or Last Island. She was one of the few survivors of a hurricane that hit the island and the southern coast of Louisiana in 1856. In those days there were no hurricane warnings. During the hurricane, she tied a scapular to a post, held on to the post, and floated out into the Gulf of Mexico. She washed ashore after the storm and was found by a doctor, whom she later married. The family nicknamed her ''Floating Island'' (page 146).

These pear preserves are very good when spread on hot biscuits (page 124) for breakfast. They also make an equally good dessert when served with Cheddar cheese and crackers.

    4   pounds hard pears, stemmed, peeled, cored, and cut
          into eighths
    4   cups sugar
    ¼   cup water
    ½   lemon, thinly sliced and seeded
    1   teaspoon apple cider vinegar
    ½   cup pineapple chunks, drained (optional)

Put all the ingredients in a heavy 3-quart pot. Cook over medium heat for 10 minutes, stirring occasionally. The sugar will liquefy. Lower the heat and simmer, uncovered, for 2 to 3 hours, stirring occasionally.

Let the preserves cool and pour them into jars with tight-fitting lids. Make sure the pears are covered with syrup. Store in the refrigerator. Any excess syrup can be used for pancakes, waffles, or Lost Bread (page 123).

   Yield: 3 pints.

BREADS

I can remember afternoon excursions on the St. Charles Avenue streetcar to buy fresh bread. It was a thrill to ride on what is still today one of the longest continuous-running electric trolley systems in the world. From uptown to downtown, under the oak-lined avenue, I listened to the clatter of the streetcar rails and the clangs of its bells as it crossed street intersections. As soon as the trolley arrived at Canal Street, I descended from its stairs and raced across the neutral ground and through the French Quarter. Elated, I entered the old French Market Grocery on Decatur Street and basked in the wide assortment of foods and produce. I bought enough fresh bread to take home for the family that night and an extra loaf for myself to consume on the trip back.

Pull-Apart Cinnamon Bread

Children love this bread because they can pull it apart by hand. It is similar in taste to the cinnamon rolls found at McKenzie's Pastry Shoppes in New Orleans. Pull-Apart Cinnamon Bread is delicious and decorative for Sunday brunches.

½ cup dark raisins
¼ cup water
2 tablespoons unbleached white flour
½ ounce active dry yeast
1 cup granulated sugar
½ cup warm water (110 to 115 degrees)
1 cup milk
16 tablespoons butter or margarine at room temperature
1 tablespoon salt
3 eggs
2 egg yolks
8 cups unbleached white flour, sifted twice
2 teaspoons vegetable oil
½ cup dark brown sugar
6 tablespoons butter or margarine, melted

Heat the raisins with ¼ cup of water in a small saucepan over low heat until the water boils up. The raisins should be puffy. Set aside.

Sprinkle the 2 tablespoons of white flour on a large cutting board and set it aside.

In a large mixing bowl, combine the yeast, granulated sugar, and warm water. Stir and set aside to let the yeast and sugar dissolve.

Heat the milk in a saucepan until it scalds. Remove the milk from the heat and add 8 tablespoons of the butter and the salt. Stir until the butter is completely melted.

Add the milk mixture to the yeast mixture. Stir in the eggs and egg yolks. Whisk for a few minutes to get the lumps out. Add 6 cups of the flour, 1 cup at a time, and beat thoroughly with a large spoon. The dough will become very sticky.

Put the dough on the floured cutting board. Use a large spatula to lift the dough and fold it over. Continue this, adding more flour until the dough is no longer sticky. Knead for 10 minutes, or until the dough is elastic and pliable. Add a little more flour, as necessary, during the kneading to keep the dough from sticking.

Shape the dough into a ball. Oil a large bowl with 1 teaspoon of the oil and place the dough in the bowl. Cover with a towel and set in a draft-free, warm (75- to 80-degree) place. Let rise for 2 hours.

Punch the dough down and let it rest for 5 minutes. Turn the dough onto a lightly floured board and shape into a ball. Let rest for 10 minutes. Oil a 10- by 6-inch tube pan.

In a small saucepan, melt the remaining 8 tablespoons of butter and add the brown sugar. Stir until dissolved. Add the drained raisins and stir.

Pinch off the dough to form 2-inch-diameter balls. Roll the balls in the raisin mixture to coat them completely. Place the balls in the bottom of the greased tube pan. Repeat the process until all of the dough is used. The balls should be arranged in loose layers. Pour the 6 tablespoons of melted butter over the top of the balls. Cover the pan with a towel and let rise in a warm place for 2 hours.

Preheat the oven to 375 degrees and bake for about 1 hour. During the baking, place a baking sheet underneath the pan to catch any dough that may drop. When done, tap the top of the bread; it should sound hollow. Invert the pan onto a serving platter or a wooden board and remove the bread from the pan. Serve hot or let it cool. It can be pulled apart or sliced. If desired, serve with butter.

Yield: 12 servings.

Jalapeño Corn Bread

In the 1920s the family had a nurse who was famous for her corn bread. All of the relatives and friends knew and loved her. She always wore a long skirt with a full petticoat underneath, gold loop earrings, and a tignon (head-scarf). For parties, regardless of the menu, she made her corn bread. When guests gathered in the dining room, she joined them. When she felt it was the right time, she went to the kitchen and brought her corn bread to the table. A meal was never complete without it.

1½	cups stone-ground yellow cornmeal
1	cup unbleached white flour
1	teaspoon salt
3	teaspoons baking powder
⅔	cup condensed milk
3	eggs, beaten
½	cup canned golden kernel corn, drained
¼	cup minced onion
4	bottled jalapeño peppers, drained, split, seeded, and minced
4	ounces sharp Cheddar cheese, grated (This equals about 1¼ cups grated cheese.)
¼	cup oil

Preheat the oven to 300 degrees.

Mix the cornmeal, flour, salt, and baking powder in a large bowl. Add the condensed milk, eggs, corn, onion, and peppers. Mix thoroughly. Place the cheese in a separate bowl.

Heat the oil in a 10-inch cast-iron skillet. Coat the sides and bottom of skillet with the hot oil and turn off the heat. Pour the oil remaining in the skillet into the batter. Mix thoroughly.

Spread half of the batter in the hot skillet. Sprinkle half of the cheese on top. Spread the remaining batter and then sprinkle on the remaining cheese.

Bake for 1 hour, or until golden brown. Cool for 10 minutes; then remove from the skillet and cool on a wire rack. Serve warm. This bread freezes well.

Yield: 8 servings.

Variation
For a sweeter Corn Bread, add ¼ cup condensed milk.

Whole Wheat–Honey Bread

1½ cups warm water (110 to 115 degrees)
¾   ounce active dry yeast
1   cup milk
½   cup honey
1   tablespoon salt
¼   cup plus 2 tablespoons vegetable oil
8   cups whole wheat flour, sifted
¼   cup unbleached white flour

Put the warm water and yeast into a large mixing bowl. Stir until dissolved and set aside.

In a small pot, heat the milk to scalding. Remove from the heat and add the honey. Stir until it has dissolved. Add the milk and honey, salt, and ¼ cup oil to the yeast mixture. Mix thoroughly and set aside for a few minutes.

Add 6 cups of the whole wheat flour, 1 cup at a time, and stir in a circular motion until the batter is thick. Then stir for 4 minutes. The dough will be sticky. Slowly stir in 1 more cup of flour. Put the dough on a board sprinkled with the ¼ cup white flour and knead. Slowly add 1 more cup of whole wheat flour during the kneading. Keep hands and board floured. Knead for 10 minutes.

Oil a large bowl with a tablespoon of oil and place the dough in the bowl. Place a damp cloth over the top to prevent the dough from drying. Set in a warm (75- to 80-degree) draft-free place and let rise for 1 hour.

Punch the dough down and redampen the cloth. Cover and let rise for 30 minutes in a warm place.

On a floured board, knead the dough for 3 minutes. Cut into 2 loaves. Place the dough in two loaf pans spread with the remaining vegetable oil. Cover the pans with a towel and let rise in a warm place for 1 hour.

Preheat the oven to 350 degrees.

Make 2 diagonal slits, about ½ inch deep, on top of each loaf. Bake for 50 to 60 minutes. The tops should be golden brown and the loaves should sound hollow when tapped on the top. Remove the loaves from the pans and cool on wire racks.

Yield: 2 loaves; 10 servings.

Lost Bread

At our house, Lost Bread, also called *Pain Perdu* or French Toast, was a Saturday breakfast special. It was usually served with hot sausage. When friends spent the night on Fridays, my mother enticed us to go to sleep by saying, "If you go to sleep now, we'll have Lost Bread in the morning." It usually worked: we went to sleep quickly with sweet dreams, and woke in the morning to the wafting aroma of Lost Bread.

2   eggs, beaten
2   cups milk
½   cup granulated sugar
2   teaspoons pure vanilla extract
2   to 4 tablespoons butter or margarine
8   slices stale bread (Use thick-sliced French, whole wheat, white, raisin, rye, or any of your choice. Fresh bread can be used, but stale is the best.)

Topping
½   cup confectioner's sugar, or 1 cup hot cane or maple syrup

Mix the eggs, milk, granulated sugar, and vanilla thoroughly in a bowl. Heat two large skillets and add 1 tablespoon of butter to each skillet.

Preheat the oven to 300 degrees.

When the skillets are hot and coated with the butter, lower the heat. Dip the bread, 1 slice at a time, into the egg mixture. Thoroughly soak the bread by turning it over about four times in the mixture. Place 2 slices in each skillet.

Raise the heat to medium and cook the bread until it is golden brown. Flip the bread and cook on the other side until it is golden brown, about 2½ minutes on each side. Place the cooked bread in a roasting pan. Cover and keep warm in the oven. Repeat the process until all of the bread has been cooked. If necessary, add a little more butter to the skillets.

To serve, place 2 slices on each plate and sprinkle with the confectioner's sugar, or pour hot cane or maple syrup on top.

Yield: 8 slices; 4 servings.

Lilly's Biscuits

Every Sunday morning we had hot fresh biscuits with home-made fig or pear preserves (pages 115 and 116).

       2   cups plus 3 tablespoons unbleached white flour
       ½   teaspoon salt
       3   teaspoons baking powder
       4   tablespoons shortening
       1   cup milk

Preheat the oven to 450 degrees.

   Put the 2 cups of flour, salt, and baking powder in a large mixing bowl. Add the shortening. Use a pastry blender to cut the shortening into the flour until the mixture is crumbly. Make a well in the flour mixture and pour the milk into the well. Stir with a fork until combined.

   Sprinkle the 3 tablespoons of flour on a pastry board. Put the dough on the board and knead it gently for 30 seconds. Roll out to a ½-inch thickness with a lightly floured rolling pin. Cut with a biscuit cutter or juice glass. Transfer the biscuits to an un-greased baking sheet. Bake for 12 to 15 minutes, or until golden brown. Serve hot.

   Yield: 20 to 24 biscuits; 8 servings.

Note: The dough can be stored in an airtight container at room temperature for 1 day after cutting and before baking.

Breadsticks

       8   ounces French bread
       ½   pound butter or margarine

Preheat the oven to 350 degrees.

   Slice the bread into 4-inch lengths. Then slice each segment in half lengthwise. Slice in half lengthwise again, so that the segments are now quartered. Set the bread aside.

Melt the butter in a 3-quart pot; then remove from the heat. Dip each piece of bread into the butter and coat all sides thoroughly. Put the bread on a jelly roll pan.

Bake for 30 minutes, or until the Breadsticks are golden brown. Let cool and serve. Breadsticks will stay fresh in an airtight container for weeks.

Yield: 24 Breadsticks; 6 servings.

Croutons

3   slices whole wheat bread
2   tablespoons butter or margarine
2   tablespoons olive oil

Preheat the oven to 300 degrees.

Cut the bread into ½-inch cubes. Heat the butter and olive oil in a large skillet over low heat. When the butter has melted, add the bread cubes. Stir the cubes until all sides are well coated. Remove from the heat.

Spread the cubes on the bottom of a 9-inch pie pan. The cubes should be only one layer deep. Bake for 30 to 40 minutes, or until they are golden brown and dry looking. Toss once after the first 15 minutes. Remove from the oven and cool. Serve or store in an airtight container for weeks. Croutons are delicious sprinkled on salads and soups.

Yield: 1 cup; 4 servings.

DESSERTS

In the 1920s, one could hear the calls of street vendors in the French Quarter as they sold their produce from mule-drawn wagons: "Watermelon!!! . . . red to the rind!" "Bananas!!! . . . Banana lady!" "Blackberries!!! . . . Blackberries!" Today, folks enjoy walking in the Quarter. They can hear jazz in neighborhood bars, glance in shop windows that line the streets, or watch tapdancers and musicians perform on sidewalks. Cafés and pastry shops permeate the air with smells of freshly baked cakes, pies, and pastries.

Pat's Mardi Gras King Cake

King Cake is a brioche-style cake shaped in an oval ring. Sugar coated in the Mardi Gras colors of purple, gold, and green, the cake is enjoyed at family meals and at parties during the Carnival season. It is served from the twelfth day after Christmas until Mardi Gras Day and commemorates the religious day, Epiphany Day, on which the Three Kings brought gifts to the infant Jesus.

Every year in New Orleans on this twelfth day, there is the Twelfth Night Revelers Carnival Ball. Small boxes are hidden in a large papier-mâché cake. Guests receive a delicious piece of cake in a box. Each maid in the court is given a box containing a large bean, which is shaped like a red bean. Every bean is silver except for one that is gold. The person who receives the gold bean becomes queen of the ball.

According to Donald Entringer, president of McKenzie's Pastry Shoppes, the King Cake originated in France. It was first sold in New Orleans in the early 1900s. Back in those days, there were over five hundred French bakeries in the city. People did not have a lot of money, so a very simple, sugar-coated French bread–style King Cake was baked. Traditionally, a small object, such as a coin, ring, large bean, or pecan, was baked into the cake. The small object was dangerous because it could be swallowed accidentally. So, a porcelain bisque doll came into use instead. In those days, the dolls cost a penny each. Stores sold about five cakes per day. Then the dolls became too expensive, so a small plastic pink baby was used as it is still used today. In the 1950s, McKenzie's started advertising King Cakes on New Orleans television, and sales increased to twenty-five cakes a day. Now, the total daily sales for all of their stores is over 5,000 cakes.

King Cake party customs have varied through the decades. I best remember the parties we had in high school. Every day for lunch, the class had a King Cake party. The person who got the piece of cake with the pink baby had to bring a King Cake the next day. The practice of the game became such an art that if the knife accidentally hit the baby, whoever got the piece with the head of the baby in it had to bring the next cake.

King Cakes come in a variety of shapes, styles, and sizes.

Pat's Mardi Gras King Cake is a traditional, simple brioche cake found in many bakeries. Whether in New Orleans or around the world, King Cake conjures the spirit of Mardi Gras and makes any meal a festive occasion. Café Brûlot Diabolique (page 158) is fabulous to accompany this culinary delight.

½	ounce dry active yeast
1	cup plus 1 teaspoon sugar
⅔	cup warm water (110 to 115 degrees)
4	tablespoons butter or margarine
1	cup milk
1½	teaspoons salt
	Rind of 1 lemon, grated
2	eggs at room temperature, lightly beaten
5	to 6 cups unbleached white flour
2	teaspoons oil
1	unshelled pecan or large nut
1	egg yolk, beaten
1	tablespoon green decorator sugar crystals
1	tablespoon gold decorator sugar crystals
1	tablespoon purple decorator sugar crystals

Dissolve the yeast and 1 teaspoon sugar in the warm water in a large bowl. Melt the butter in a saucepan over medium heat. Add the 1 cup sugar, milk, salt, and grated lemon rind. Stir until the sugar is completely dissolved. Do not boil. Add to the yeast mixture and blend in thoroughly.

Add the eggs to the yeast mixture. Stir lightly. Beat in 2 cups of the flour with a wire whisk until the dough is smooth and not lumpy, about 2 minutes. Use a spoon to gradually stir in 3 more cups of the flour until the dough is stiff. Turn the dough out onto a floured board.

Add the remaining flour and knead until the dough is smooth and elastic, about 8 to 10 minutes. Place the dough in a greased bowl. Turn the dough to grease all sides of the dough. Cover with a damp towel. Place the dough in a warm (80- to 90-degree), draft-free place. Let rise until it is double in bulk, about 1 to 1½ hours.

Punch the dough down. Put it on a lightly floured board. Let rest for 10 minutes. Stretch the dough into a long, 36-inch rope.

Shape the rope into a large oval on a greased baking sheet. Pinch the ends together to seal. Lift a small section of the dough and push the pecan into the dough from underneath. Pinch the dough underneath the pecan so that it is covered. Place a damp towel over the dough. Let rise in a warm, draft-free place for about 1 hour, or until it is double in bulk.

Preheat the oven to 350 degrees.

Very carefully brush the risen dough with egg yolk. Sprinkle the decorator sugars generously on top in 2-inch bands of alternating colors (to make superfine sugar crystals, blend each color separately in a blender for 60 seconds).

Bake for 30 to 40 minutes. Tap the cake lightly on the bottom with your fingertips. When the cake is done, it will sound hollow. Be very careful not to overcook and burn the bottom of the King Cake.

Carefully remove the cake from the baking sheet. Cool on a wire rack. Serve warm or at room temperature. Don't forget, the person who gets the piece of cake with the pecan must give the next party.

Yield: one 14-inch cake or two 12-inch cakes;
12 servings.

Note: High humidity affects the stickiness of the dough and may necessitate a longer initial kneading time or the use of a little more flour. Cold weather may slow the rising process. Under these conditions, let the dough rise in an unlit oven with a pilot light.

Variation

To make 2 small cakes, cut the dough in half and make two 30-inch-long ropes. Place each piece of dough on a separate greased baking sheet. Shape into an oval ring and hide an unshelled pecan in each cake. Continue, following the directions.

Cocoa Cake

Cake

¾ cup plus 2 teaspoons butter or margarine at room
  temperature
1¾ cups granulated sugar
2 eggs
1 teaspoon pure vanilla extract
2 cups whole wheat flour, sifted twice
¾ cup plus 2 teaspoons unsweetened cocoa powder
1¼ teaspoons baking soda
½ teaspoon salt
1⅓ cups water

Frosting

¾ cup unsweetened cocoa powder
2⅔ cups confectioner's sugar
6 tablespoons butter or margarine at room temperature
5 to 6 tablespoons milk
1 teaspoon pure vanilla extract

To make the cake, preheat the oven to 350 degrees.

Put the ¾ cup butter and the sugar in a large mixing bowl and cream until light and fluffy. Add the eggs, vanilla, flour, ¾ cup cocoa, baking soda, salt, and water. Beat for 2 minutes with an electric mixer on medium speed. Set the batter aside.

Use the 2 teaspoons of butter to grease two 9-inch pie pans. Dust the pie pans with the remaining 2 teaspoons of cocoa. Pour equal amounts of the cake batter into each pan. Bake for 30 to 35 minutes. Cool the cakes in the pans for 10 minutes; then remove the cakes from the pans and cool completely on wire racks.

To prepare the frosting, combine the cocoa and sugar in a small bowl. In another bowl, cream the butter with ½ cup of the cocoa mixture. Add the remaining cocoa mixture and the milk. Beat to a spreading consistency; then stir in the vanilla.

When the cakes are thoroughly cool, put one cake on a serving platter. Spread some of the frosting on top of the cake. Place the other cake on top of the frosting and spread the remaining frosting over the top and sides of the cake.

Yield: 8 servings.

Lemon Yum-Yum Cake

Cake

1 cup plus 2 teaspoons butter or margarine at room
temperature
1½ cups sugar
4 eggs
4 teaspoons baking powder
3 cups plus 2 teaspoons unbleached white flour, sifted
½ teaspoon salt
1 cup milk at room temperature
2 teaspoons pure vanilla extract

Filling

½ cup butter or margarine, melted
½ cup sugar
1 tablespoon unbleached white flour
1 teaspoon ground cinnamon
½ cup chopped pecans

Topping

5 eggs, well beaten
1⅔ cups sugar
1½ tablespoons fresh lemon juice
2 tablespoons grated lemon rind

Preheat the oven to 325 degrees.

To prepare the cake batter, cream the 1 cup of butter and the
sugar in a large bowl. Add the eggs, 1 at a time, beating well
after each addition.

Sift the baking powder, 3 cups flour, and salt together and add
to the butter mixture. Add the milk and vanilla and mix well.

Use the 2 teaspoons of butter to grease two 9-inch cake pans.
Dust the pans with the remaining 2 teaspoons of flour. Pour
equal amounts of the cake batter into each pan. Bake for 45 to
50 minutes. Cool the cakes in the pans for 5 minutes; then remove the cakes from the pans and cool completely on wire
racks.

To prepare the filling, mix all of the filling ingredients in a
large bowl. Set aside until needed.

To prepare the topping, put the eggs, sugar, lemon juice, and lemon rind into a medium-sized saucepan. Mix thoroughly. Then put the pan over low heat and stir constantly for 7 to 10 minutes, or until the mixture thickens. (Make sure the eggs do not cook too fast.) Remove the pan from the heat.

When the cakes are thoroughly cool, put one cake on a serving platter. Spread all of the filling on the top of the cake, covering it completely. Place the other layer on top of the filling. Spread the topping over the top and sides of the cake. Refrigerate the cake and serve cold or at room temperature.

Yield: 8 servings.

Cheesecake with Strawberry Glaze

Crust

9	ounces vanilla wafers
¼	cup chopped pecans
¼	cup sugar
8	tablespoons butter or margarine, melted

Filling

3	8-ounce packages cream cheese at room temperature
1	cup sugar
4	eggs
2	teaspoons pure vanilla extract
½	cup light cream

Topping

16	ounces sour cream
¾	cup sugar
1	teaspoon pure vanilla extract

Glaze

3	1-pint boxes fresh strawberries
½	cup boiling water
2	tablespoons cornstarch
½	cup sugar

To prepare the crust, put the vanilla wafers in the container of a blender. Blend the wafers on medium speed until they are ground. (You may have to blend the wafers in several batches.) Pour the ground wafers into a large bowl. Add the remaining crust ingredients and mix well. Pat the crust over the bottom and sides of two 9-inch pie pans.

Preheat the oven to 350 degrees.

To prepare the filling, put all the filling ingredients in a medium-sized bowl. Blend with an electric mixer on medium speed until smooth. Spread equal amounts of the filling over the crust in the two pie pans. Bake for 30 to 40 minutes, or until the tops look dry. Remove from the oven and cool for 30 minutes.

Preheat the oven to 400 degrees.

To make the topping, mix all the topping ingredients together in a small bowl. Spread equal amounts of the mixture on each cake. Bake for 5 to 10 minutes. Remove from the oven and cool completely. Then refrigerate for at least 1 hour before glazing the cakes. (The Cheesecake freezes well at this point.)

To make the glaze, hull, wash, and drain the strawberries. Set aside 15 of the largest berries to decorate the finished Cheesecakes. Put the remaining strawberries into a pan with the boiling water and cook for 10 minutes, or until the berries are very mushy. Pass the berries through a colander or strainer into a bowl. Return the purée to the pan and put it over low heat.

Mix the cornstarch and sugar together in a small bowl. Then add the mixture to the strawberry purée, stirring constantly. When the purée comes to a boil, boil for 1 minute. Remove the pan from the heat and let the glaze cool. Transfer the glaze to a bowl, cover, and refrigerate for 2 hours before glazing the cakes.

To serve, slice the 15 reserved whole strawberries in half. Use them to decorate the tops of the cakes. Pour the glaze over the top of the cakes and refrigerate the cakes until serving time. (Do not freeze the glaze.)

Yield: two 9-inch Cheesecakes; 10 servings.

Alexis' Cocoons

Cocoons are especially fun for children to make because they can mold them by hand.

When I was young and spent the night at the home of my friend Alexis, we always made Cocoons. We usually ate half of the dough before it was baked (that was part of the fun); then we polished off the Cocoons as soon as they came out of the oven.

2¼   cups unbleached white flour
1⅓   cups confectioner's sugar
½   pound shelled pecans, chopped
½   pound butter or margarine, melted
1   tablespoon vegetable oil

Preheat the oven to 350 degrees.

Put the flour, ⅔ cup of the sugar, and the pecans in a large mixing bowl. Mix thoroughly. Add the melted butter and mix it in with your hand.

Spread the oil on two baking sheets.

Use about 1½ tablespoons of the dough to make each Cocoon, molding it into a cocoon or oval shape by hand. Put the cookies on the baking sheets.

Bake for 30 minutes, or until the bottoms of the cookies are light brown. Do not overbake. Cool the cookies completely on wire racks.

Pour the remaining ⅔ cup sugar into a plastic bag. Drop 5 or 6 cookies into the bag and toss to cover them completely with the sugar. Place the cookies on a platter to serve. The Cocoons will keep for about 2 weeks in an airtight container, if you are lucky.

Yield: 4 dozen cookies; 8 servings.

Pecan Balls

½   pound butter or margarine at room temperature
6   tablespoons granulated sugar
1   teaspoon pure vanilla extract
2   cups ground shelled pecans
1½ to 2 cups unbleached white flour
1   teaspoon vegetable oil
½   cup confectioner's sugar

Preheat the oven to 350 degrees.

Cream the butter and granulated sugar in a large mixing bowl. Add the vanilla, pecans, and 1½ cups of the flour. Mix thoroughly. Continue adding flour just until the dough can be rolled into a ball.

Spread the oil on a baking sheet.

Use about 1 tablespoon of the dough to make each small ball. Place the cookies on the baking sheet.

Bake for 30 to 40 minutes, or until the bottoms of the cookies are light brown. Let the cookies cool thoroughly on wire racks.

Pour the confectioner's sugar into a plastic bag. Drop 8 or 10 cookies into the bag and toss to cover them completely with the sugar. Place the cookies on a platter to serve.

Yield: 70 to 80 cookies; 12 servings.

Apple Pie

6	to 7 medium-sized tart apples, peeled, cored, and thinly sliced
½	cup plus 1 teaspoon granulated sugar
½	cup dark brown sugar
2	tablespoons fresh lemon juice
1	teaspoon ground nutmeg
1	recipe Plain Pastry (page 143)
6	tablespoons butter or margarine

Preheat the oven to 450 degrees.

Put the apples, ½ cup granulated sugar, brown sugar, lemon juice, and nutmeg in a large bowl. Mix until the apples are thoroughly coated with the sugar and spices. Pour the apple mixture into a pastry-lined pie pan. Dot the apples with the butter.

Cut the remaining layer of pastry into ½-inch-wide strips and make a crisscross pattern on top of the apples in the pie pan. Crimp the edges of the pastry together. Sprinkle the remaining teaspoon of sugar over the top of the pie.

Put the pie pan on a large baking sheet with sides. Transfer the baking sheet with the pie plate to the oven and bake for 15 minutes. Lower the oven temperature to 350 degrees and bake for 50 minutes longer. The apples should be soft and light brown when they are done. Remove from the oven and serve the pie hot or cold.

For an extra treat, serve the pie à la mode with a scoop of good-quality vanilla ice cream on top; or you can melt a slice of Cheddar cheese on top of the hot pie.

Yield: 8 servings.

Variation

For a spicier filling, you can add 1 teaspoon ground cinnamon, ¼ teaspoon ground allspice, and 1 tablespoon unbleached white flour to the apple mixture.

Blackberry Pie

A few decades ago the street songs of the Blackberry Lady could be heard on Saturday mornings. Chanting "Blaaack Berrries," she came to the open kitchen door and held up a large straw basket full of freshly picked berries wrapped in a large white cloth. With a clear glass she measured cups of berries and poured them into a bowl. They were soon devoured for breakfast with fresh cream or were baked in a pie. In the 1930s, the chant was "Blaaaack Berries! . . . Blackberries, Blaaaaaack Berries, fresh and fine, just took em' off de vine, only cost a dime, please get 'em all de time!"

      4   cups fresh blackberries, washed and drained
      1   cup plus ½ teaspoon sugar
  1½   tablespoons fresh lemon juice
      1   teaspoon grated lemon rind
      4   tablespoons unbleached white flour
   ⅛   teaspoon salt
      1   recipe Plain Pastry (page 143)
      1   teaspoon butter or margarine

Preheat the oven to 450 degrees.

Put the blackberries, 1 cup sugar, lemon juice, lemon rind, flour, and salt in a large bowl. Mix well. Pour the berry mixture into a pastry-lined pie pan. Dot berry mixture with the butter.

Cut the remaining layer of pastry into ½-inch-wide strips and make a crisscross pattern on top of the berries in the pie pan. Crimp the edges of the pastry together. Sprinkle the remaining ½ teaspoon of sugar over the top of the pie.

Put the pie pan on a large baking sheet with sides. Transfer the baking sheet with the pie pan to the oven and bake for 10 minutes. Lower the oven temperature to 350 degrees and bake for 50 to 60 minutes longer, or until the crust is golden brown. Let the pie cool before serving.

Yield: 6 servings.

Variation

For Raspberry Pie, substitute 4 cups of fresh raspberries for the blackberries.

Lemon Meringue Pie

Filling
1½ cups sugar
5 tablespoons cornstarch
¼ teaspoon salt
1½ cups boiling water
3 egg yolks
⅓ cup fresh lemon juice
1 tablespoon grated lemon rind
6 tablespoons butter or margarine

Meringue
3 tablespoons sugar
3 egg whites at room temperature

Crust
½ recipe Plain Pastry (page 143), baked

To prepare the filling, combine the sugar, cornstarch, and salt in a large saucepan. Cook over low heat, stirring constantly, for a few minutes. Gradually add the boiling water to the saucepan. Cook for 1 or 2 minutes, or until the sugar and cornstarch are completely dissolved. Set aside.

Beat the egg yolks in a bowl. Pour some of the hot syrup over the egg yolks and beat vigorously. Do not let the yolks overcook. Pour the egg yolk mixture into the saucepan with the syrup and cook for 2 minutes, stirring constantly. Remove from the heat and add the lemon juice, lemon rind, and butter. Blend thoroughly and then beat well. Let the custard cool.

To prepare the meringue, combine the sugar and egg whites in a bowl. Use an electric mixer to beat the egg whites until they are stiff. Set aside until needed.

Preheat the oven to broil.

Pour the cooled lemon custard into the baked piecrust. Spread the meringue on top of the custard. Broil for 30 to 60 seconds, or until the meringue is golden brown. Watch carefully so that the meringue does not burn. Remove the pie from the oven. Serve hot or cold. Store in the refrigerator.

Yield: 6 servings.

Vinson's Pecan Pie

1	16-ounce bottle dark karo syrup
6	eggs
1	cup sugar
1	teaspoon pure vanilla extract
1½	cups shelled whole pecans
1	recipe Plain Pastry (page 143)
2	tablespoons butter or margarine

Preheat the oven to 325 degrees.

Remove the cap from the bottle of syrup and heat the syrup in a small saucepan of water.

Put the eggs, sugar, vanilla, and hot syrup in a large mixing bowl. Stir to mix thoroughly.

Pour the filling equally into two prepared pastry shells. Sprinkle ¾ cup of the pecans into each pie. Dot each pie with 1 tablespoon of the butter.

Put the pies on a large baking sheet with sides. Transfer the baking sheet with the pie pans to the oven and bake for 1 hour. Remove from the oven and cool. Serve warm or at room temperature. Store in the refrigerator.

Yield: 10 servings.

Apple Cream Tart

Pastry
½   cup butter or margarine at room temperature
⅓   cup sugar
¼   teaspoon pure vanilla extract
1   cup unbleached white flour
½   cup finely chopped walnuts
1   teaspoon vegetable oil

Apples
½   cup dark raisins
⅓   cup water
2   pounds firm apples, peeled, cored, and thinly sliced
⅓   cup sugar
½   teaspoon ground cinnamon

Filling
8   ounces cream cheese at room temperature
¼   cup sugar
1   egg
½   teaspoon pure vanilla extract

½   cup chopped walnuts or pecans

To prepare the pastry, cream the butter, sugar, and vanilla in a mixing bowl. Add the flour and nuts and mix well.

Spread the oil over the bottom and sides of a 9-inch spring-form pan. Spread the pastry on the bottom and about halfway up the sides of the pan. Set aside until needed.

To prepare the apples, simmer the raisins in the water for 2 minutes, or until the raisins are puffy and the water has evaporated. Remove the pan from the heat and pour the raisins into a large mixing bowl. Add the apples, sugar, and cinnamon. Mix thoroughly and set aside.

Preheat the oven to 450 degrees.

Put all of the filling ingredients in a mixing bowl. Use an electric mixer on medium speed to blend until smooth. Spread the filling evenly over the pastry. Spoon the apple mixture gently over the filling. Then sprinkle with the nuts.

Place a jelly roll pan on a separate rack under the springform pan. Bake for 10 minutes. Lower the oven temperature to 400 degrees and bake for 25 minutes longer. (If using very hard apples, cook 90 minutes longer.) Remove the tart from the oven and cool in the pan before removing the sides of the pan. Serve warm or at room temperature.

Yield: 6 servings.

Plain Pastry

3½ cups plus 3 tablespoons unbleached white flour
2   eggs
½   teaspoon salt
½   pound butter or margarine at room temperature
2   tablespoons cold water, if needed

Put the 3½ cups of flour on a clean counter top. Make a well in the center of the flour and put the eggs, salt, and butter into the well. Working from the center, slowly mix the ingredients by hand. Work the dough with the palm of your hand, pushing it downward until the dough is no longer sticky. Add a little water, if necessary, to keep the dough together. After a few minutes the dough should come away from the counter top and no longer be sticky.

Put the dough in a bowl, cover, and refrigerate until cool.

When ready to use, roll out half of the dough on a board sprinkled with the 3 tablespoons of flour to a thickness of ⅛ inch. Transfer the dough to the pie pan and use as directed in the recipe.

For recipes using a baked crust, prepare the dough as directed. Then prick the dough in the pan all over with a fork. Bake in a 400-degree oven for 15 to 20 minutes, or until it is light brown. Remove from the oven and cool before filling.

Yield: two 9-inch pastry crusts.

Variation

For dessert crusts, add ⅓ cup sugar to the flour before mixing it with the other ingredients.

Crème Brûlée

Pronounced KREHM brew-LAY, the words translated from the French mean "burnt cream." This is a rich custard with a caramelized glaze. It takes two days to prepare.

Day 1
    4   cups heavy cream
    8   egg yolks
    5   tablespoons granulated sugar
    2   teaspoons pure vanilla extract

Day 2
    ½   cup dark brown sugar

Day 1: Heat the cream in a 2-quart saucepan until it begins to scald. Remove from the heat.

Put the egg yolks and sugar in a large bowl and use a wire whisk to blend them thoroughly. While continuing to whisk, pour the hot cream into the bowl very slowly. Then add the vanilla and mix well.

Preheat the oven to 350 degrees.

Pour the custard into a 1½-quart baking dish. Put the baking dish in a larger roasting pan. Pour in enough hot water to come halfway up the side of the baking dish. Bake for 2 hours. Remove from the oven and roasting pan and cool the custard completely. Cover and refrigerate overnight.

Day 2: Preheat the oven to broil. Remove the baked custard from refrigerator. Place the baking dish in a larger roasting pan filled with ice and water. Sprinkle the brown sugar over custard.

Place the baking dish in the roasting pan under the broiler for about 2 minutes. Keep the door to the broiler open. Carefully turn the baking dish around every 20 seconds. Do not let the sugar burn. When the sugar is caramelized, remove the custard from the broiler. Let it stand for 5 minutes; then remove the baking dish from the roasting pan. Dry off the sides of the baking dish and serve at once. Or cover and refrigerate until serving time. The custard should be served within a few hours.

Yield: 6 servings.

Variation
Crème Brûlée is delicious when served with sliced fresh fruit, such as peaches and plums.

Cup Custard

     3   eggs
    ½   cup sugar
     2   cups milk
    1½   teaspoons pure vanilla extract
    ½   teaspoon vegetable oil
    1½   teaspoons freshly grated nutmeg

Put the eggs and sugar in a bowl and beat until creamy.

Heat the milk to the scalding point. Pour the milk very slowly into the egg mixture, beating constantly. Stir in the vanilla.

Preheat the oven to 350 degrees.

Spread the oil over the bottom and sides of a 1-quart baking dish or four individual baking cups. Pour the custard through a strainer into the baking dish or cups. Sprinkle the top of the custard heavily with the nutmeg. Place the baking dish or cups in a large roasting pan. Pour in enough hot water to come half-way up the side of the dish or cups.

Bake for 1 to 1½ hours. (Individual baking cups will take only 25 to 30 minutes.) The custard is done when a knife inserted in the custard comes out clean. Remove the custard from the oven and cool. Cover and refrigerate and serve cold.

   Yield: 4 servings.

Floating Island

Many decades ago, it was a tradition in my family to trim the Christmas tree on Christmas Eve. After dinner, the candles on the tree were lit and the adults had eggnog and fruitcake. The children were served Floating Island and stuffed dates. Floating Island is also called *Les Oeufs à la Neige* or *Les Îles Flottantes*.

In southern France, most people eat fresh fruit or simple desserts, instead of heavy desserts, with their meals. Floating Island is one of the most typical desserts served at home for their Sunday dinners.

Children love to help make this dessert. It's fun for them to stir the sauce and watch the egg whites puff. When serving, it is usually a contest to see who can get the most islands.

6	eggs at room temperature
¼	cup granulated sugar
6	cups milk
½	teaspoon pure vanilla extract
⅛	teaspoon ground cinnamon
1	tablespoon confectioner's sugar

Separate the eggs and put the yolks in one bowl and the whites in another. Mix the egg yolks with the sugar. Whisk for a few minutes until the mixture becomes pale yellow and foamy. Set aside.

In a heavy saucepan over medium heat, bring 4 cups of the milk, the vanilla, and cinnamon to a scald. Be careful not to boil the milk; it should just simmer with a little vapor rising from the top. Stir occasionally with a wire whisk to keep the milk from sticking to the bottom of the pan.

Slowly pour the hot milk into the egg yolk mixture, stirring constantly. Do not let egg yolks get lumpy. Pour the mixture back into the saucepan and put the pan over low heat. With a wooden spoon, stir continuously for about 20 minutes. The sauce is ready when the foam on the surface disappears and the sauce thickens enough to lightly coat the spoon. Do not let the mixture boil. It should be the consistency of a custard sauce, not a pudding.

The sauce is now a *crème anglaise*. Pour the sauce into a large flat-bottomed 3-quart dish. Let cool to room temperature.

Use an electric mixer to beat the egg whites until they are very firm and can hold a peak. Gently fold the confectioner's sugar into the whites.

Pour the remaining 2 cups of milk into a large heavy skillet. Bring to a boil. Lower the heat so that the milk stays at a simmer. Carefully drop 1 tablespoon of the egg white mixture into the milk. Poach it for 2 minutes on each side. Using a large slotted spoon, turn the meringue over. You can poach more than 1 egg white ball at a time, but don't crowd them. The whites tend to expand while they poach and stick to each other if they are too close. Do 6 to 8 meringues at a time.

Spoon the poached whites onto a cloth towel to drain. When the *crème anglaise* is cool, place the whites on top; they will appear to be floating islands.

Floating Island can be made up to 3 hours in advance and refrigerated.

Yield: 6 servings.

Bread Pudding with Whiskey Sauce

4   cups milk
2   cups stale French bread cut into 1-inch cubes
¾   cup sugar
1   tablespoon butter or margarine
¼   teaspoon salt
4   eggs, beaten
1   teaspoon pure vanilla extract
½   teaspoon ground cinnamon
½   teaspoon ground nutmeg
½   teaspoon vegetable oil
1   cup dark raisins

Whiskey Sauce
1½   cups heavy cream
⅓   cup sugar
¼   cup bourbon

Preheat the oven to 350 degrees.

Scald the milk in a large saucepan; then remove from the heat. Stir the bread into the milk and let it soak for 5 minutes. Then stir in the sugar, butter, salt, eggs, vanilla, cinnamon, and nutmeg.

Spread the oil over the bottom and sides of a 1½-quart baking dish. Pour the custard mixture into the baking dish and sprinkle the raisins on top. (The raisins will sink to the bottom if they are stirred too much.)

Put the baking dish in a larger roasting pan and pour in enough hot water to come halfway up the side of the baking dish. Bake for 1 to 1½ hours. Add more hot water to the roasting pan, if necessary. The custard is done when a knife inserted in the custard comes out clean.

To prepare the sauce, pour the cream into a chilled bowl and beat until stiff using an electric mixer on high speed. Add the sugar and continue beating until it is well blended. Whisk in the bourbon, cover the bowl, and refrigerate the sauce until needed.

When the pudding is done, remove it from the oven. Serve the pudding hot or cold with generous spoonfuls of the Whiskey Sauce on top of each serving.
Yield: 6 servings.

Mocha Mousse

4   1-ounce squares semisweet chocolate
¼   cup strong coffee
4   egg yolks, beaten
1   to 2 tablespoons dark rum
4   egg whites at room temperature
½   cup sugar
⅛   teaspoon salt

Garnishes
½   cup heavy cream, whipped stiff
2   tablespoons minced nuts
2   tablespoons grated semisweet chocolate

Put the chocolate in a small saucepan with the coffee. Heat over low heat until the chocolate has melted. Remove from the heat and cool for 5 minutes; then briskly whisk in the egg yolks and rum. Set aside to cool completely.

Beat the egg whites in a large bowl with an electric mixer on high speed until they are fluffy. Add the sugar and salt and beat until stiff and glossy, about 1 to 2 minutes longer. (You should not be able to feel a grain of sugar on your tongue or between your fingers.)

Gently fold ½ cup of the egg whites into the cooled chocolate mixture. Pour the chocolate mixture back into the remaining egg whites and fold it in completely.

Pour the mousse into a 1-quart serving dish. Cover and refrigerate for at least 4 hours or overnight. The mousse should be very firm when it is served. Top with any or all of the garnishes.
Yield: 6 servings.

Chocolate Mousse

4	egg yolks
2	cups milk
¼	cup sugar
3	ounces semisweet chocolate, grated
¼	ounce unflavored gelatin
2	tablespoons cold water
1	cup heavy cream
1	teaspoon pure vanilla extract
2	tablespoons brandy

Put the egg yolks into a bowl. Beat them and set them aside.

Combine the milk, sugar, and chocolate in a 1-quart saucepan. Cook over low heat, stirring constantly, until the mixture begins to scald. Remove from the heat and set aside.

Whisk about ¼ cup of the hot milk mixture into the egg yolk mixture. Then whisk the egg yolk mixture slowly into the hot milk in the saucepan. Put the saucepan over low heat and cook the custard over low heat, stirring frequently, for about 15 minutes, or until the mixture thickens.

Dissolve the gelatin in the cold water and set it aside.

When the custard is thick, remove the pan from the heat and stir in the softened gelatin. Mix well and strain the mixture through a sieve into a bowl. To cool, set the bowl with the custard in a larger bowl filled with ice water. Set aside for 30 to 45 minutes. Stir the custard occasionally while it is cooling and add more ice to the larger bowl, if necessary.

After 30 minutes, pour the cream into a chilled bowl and beat until stiff using an electric mixer on high speed. Put ½ cup of the whipped cream into a small bowl, cover, and refrigerate for the topping. Add the vanilla and brandy to the remaining whipped cream. Set aside until needed.

When the chocolate mixture is thoroughly cool but still liquid, gently fold it into the whipped cream that has been flavored with the vanilla and brandy. Blend well. Pour the mousse into a serving bowl or individual custard cups. Cover and refrigerate for 2 hours. When ready to serve, dot the reserved ½ cup whipped cream over the top of the mousse.

Yield: 8 servings.

Ice Cream Balls

½   cup butter or margarine
1   pound pecan halves, shelled
1   teaspoon salt
½   gallon good-quality vanilla ice cream
1   12-ounce jar caramel sauce

Preheat the oven to 350 degrees.

Melt the butter in a large skillet. Add the pecans and stir well. Then transfer the buttered pecans to a large baking sheet. Bake for 15 minutes, stirring occasionally, until the nuts are golden brown. Remove from the oven and sprinkle the nuts with the salt. Cool.

Chop the cooled pecans and put them in a large bowl.

Cut aluminum foil into sixteen 6-inch-square sheets.

Remove the ice cream from the freezer and let it get semisoft. Scoop the ice cream into 3-inch-diameter balls and roll the balls in the chopped pecans, coating each ball thoroughly with the nuts. Quickly wrap each ice cream ball in a sheet of foil and twist the ends on top. Place the ice cream balls in the freezer to harden. (The ice cream balls can be kept in the freezer for days.)

To serve, remove the cap from the jar of caramel sauce and heat the sauce in the jar in a saucepan of boiling water. Remove the foil from the ice cream balls and put 2 on each serving plate. Pour the hot caramel sauce into a sauceboat and spoon it on top of each serving at the table.

Yield: 8 servings.

Mamou's Mocha Ice Cream Bombe

3   ounces blanched slivered almonds
8   ounces coconut macaroons (Use the fresh, moist "mound" type.)
½   gallon good-quality coffee ice cream
1   cup heavy cream
½   cup crème de cacao

Preheat the oven to 350 degrees.

Spread the almonds on a baking sheet and toast them in the oven for 5 to 10 minutes, or until they are light brown. Set them aside.

Crumble the macaroons by hand and spread them out on a baking sheet. Bake for 15 minutes; then let them cool. (The macaroons will be crisp.)

If a melon mold is available, use it. If not, use a medium-sized metal bowl.

Remove the ice cream from the freezer and let it soften for 5 to 10 minutes. Line the mold with 1 inch of the softened ice cream. Fill the cavity with the macaroon crumbs. Spread the remaining ice cream on top of the macaroons to seal the cavity. Place the lid on the mold, or a plate on the bowl, and freeze for at least 30 minutes. (The mold can be kept for days in the freezer.)

To serve, pour the cream into a chilled bowl and beat with an electric mixer until it is firm.

Remove the lid from the mold and wrap the mold in a towel that has been soaked in hot water and wrung out. Invert the mold onto a serving platter. Cover the ice cream with the whipped cream. Sprinkle the almonds over the bombe. Pour the liqueur into a small bowl. Slice the bombe and serve with spoonfuls of the liqueur on top.

Yield: 8 servings.

Corn Flake Ice Cream Ring

¾ pound butter or margarine
2 cups dark brown sugar
1 teaspoon pure almond extract
4½ cups corn flakes
½ teaspoon vegetable oil
½ gallon good-quality vanilla ice cream
1 pint fresh strawberries, hulled, washed, and halved

Melt the butter in a medium-sized saucepan. Add the brown sugar and almond extract. Boil for 2 minutes.

Put the corn flakes into a large mixing bowl. Pour the hot sauce over the corn flakes and mix thoroughly.

Spread the oil over the inside of a ring mold. Fill the mold with the corn flake mixture and pat it down firmly. Refrigerate for a few hours or overnight.

To serve, remove the ice cream from the freezer and let it soften for 5 to 10 minutes. Remove the corn flake ring from the mold by placing the mold for a minute or two in a sink with 1 or 2 inches of hot water. Dry the mold and invert it onto a serving platter. Fill the ring with ice cream. Toss the fresh strawberries on top and slice.

Yield: 8 servings.

Macaroon Ice Cream Delight

2   pounds almond macaroons (Use the fresh, moist "mound" type.)
½   gallon good-quality vanilla ice cream
3   ounces bourbon

Preheat the oven to 400 degrees.

Crumble the macaroons by hand and spread them out on two large baking sheets. Bake for 10 minutes, or until golden brown. Toss occasionally while they bake. Let the macaroons cool.

Remove the ice cream from the freezer and let it get semisoft. Put the ice cream in a large bowl. Add the cooled macaroon crumbs and mix thoroughly. Add the bourbon and blend well. Pour the mixture into two ½-gallon containers and freeze solid. Serve frozen.

Yield: 12 servings.

Minted Watermelon

The beauty of this dessert is its simplicity.

1   4-pound watermelon
2   tablespoons chopped fresh mint leaves or 2 tablespoons dried mint leaves

Use a large spoon to scoop out the flesh of the melon. Remove all seeds and cut it into bite-sized pieces. Take 1 cup of the juice remaining in the melon and strain it. Discard the rest.

Put the melon pieces, juice, and mint in a large mixing bowl. Mix thoroughly. Cover and refrigerate for at least 20 minutes before serving.

Yield: 4 to 5 cups; 6 servings.

Pears Belle Hélène

Pears

    6   large firm Bartlett pears
    ½   lemon
    2   cups water
    1   cup sugar

Chocolate Sauce

    1   cup pear syrup (from cooked pears above)
    4   1-ounce squares unsweetened chocolate

    1   8-inch yellow layer cake, prepared from a mix
    1   pint good-quality vanilla ice cream, softened slightly

Peel the pears and trim the tops and bottoms so they are flat. Sprinkle lemon juice over the pears to prevent them from discoloring. Put the pears in a bowl of cold water.

Put the 2 cups of water and the sugar in a large saucepan. Cook over medium heat, stirring frequently, for 5 minutes. Drain the pears well and add them to the syrup in the pan. Simmer the pears for 10 to 15 minutes, stirring occasionally, until they are tender when pierced with a fork. Use a slotted spoon to remove the pears from the syrup. Put them in a bowl. Continue cooking the syrup until it is reduced to 1 cup. Set the syrup aside.

Combine the 1 cup of pear syrup and the chocolate in a saucepan over low heat. Simmer, stirring frequently, for 5 to 7 minutes. Set aside and let cool. When the sauce has cooled, refrigerate it for 30 minutes to chill it, but do not let the sauce get hard.

Place the cake layer on a serving platter. Spoon the ice cream on top of the cake and spread it gently. Place the pears upright on top of the ice cream so that the small end is pointing up. Pour cooled chocolate sauce over each pear and serve the dessert immediately. Each serving should consist of cake, ice cream, pear, and sauce. Serve any extra sauce in a bowl at the table.

      Yield: 6 servings.

Mama's Pralines

Pronounced PRAW-leens, these candies are made by browning nuts in sugar.

  1½   cups dark brown sugar
  1½   cups granulated sugar
   2   tablespoons butter or margarine
  ⅛   teaspoon salt
  1½   cups evaporated milk
   2   cups shelled whole pecans
   1   teaspoon pure vanilla extract
   1   teaspoon vegetable oil

Combine all the ingredients in a large saucepan. Cook, stirring constantly with a wooden spoon, over medium heat. The mixture should be at a low boil. Make sure that the spoon touches the bottom and sides of the pan constantly. Cook at a low boil for about 4 minutes, or until a drop of the mixture forms a "hard-ball" when dropped into a cup of very cold water. (If you are using a candy thermometer, it should register 260 degrees.)

Remove the saucepan from the heat and beat the mixture briskly for 2 minutes, or until it cools, thickens, and becomes creamy.

Set out large pieces of wax paper or aluminum foil or oiled baking sheets. Form the pralines by dropping 2 or 3 pecans combined with a tablespoon of the syrup into individual mounds. Let the candies cool completely. Store in an airtight container.

Yield: 40 candies; 10 servings.

Gran's Date Nut Roll

2   cups sugar
½   cup evaporated milk
1   teaspoon pure vanilla extract
1   cup chopped shelled pecans
1   cup chopped pitted dates

Put the sugar and milk into a 2-quart saucepan. Cook over medium heat, stirring constantly, until a drop of the mixture forms
a "soft-ball" when dropped into a cup of very cold water. (If
you are using a candy thermometer, it should register 240 degrees.)

Add the vanilla, pecans, and dates, and continue cooking over
low heat for 2 minutes longer, stirring constantly. Remove from
the heat and and set aside to cool for 30 minutes.

Dampen a clean, soft cotton cloth which measures 14 by 24
inches. Spread the cloth out on a counter. Pour the mixture
along the 24-inch edge of the cloth. Roll the mixture tightly in
the cloth until it is long and smooth. The roll should measure 18
by 2 inches. Tie each end of the roll tightly with string, and
suspend the roll from a hook until the candy is firm, 6 to 12
hours.

Remove the cloth gently and cut the roll into ¼-inch-thick
slices. Store in an airtight container in the refrigerator. Serve at
room temperature.

Yield: 20 to 25 candies; 6 servings.

Note: Rinse the cloth thoroughly in warm water and then wash
it in soapy water. Rinse thoroughly, dry, and store for use at
another time.

Café Brûlot Diabolique

If a Brûlot Bowl is not available, use a fancy metal serving bowl (but not one made of silver, because silver melts). Or use the pot in which the coffee is heated. The ceremony will not be as spectacular without the Brûlot Bowl, but the excitement and taste will be the same.

1	lemon, washed
1	orange, washed
4	8-ounce cups strong black coffee, preferably a coffee and chicory blend, dripped French style
⅓	cup sugar
5	whole cloves
1	cinnamon stick
1	vanilla bean, or 2 teaspoons pure vanilla extract
¾	cup brandy, or 1 cup bourbon

Cut peels from the lemon and orange in a circular motion to create long strips. Do not include the white part under the rind.

Put the coffee, sugar, lemon and orange peels, cloves, cinnamon, and vanilla into a medium-sized saucepan. Simmer over low heat for 10 minutes, but do not allow the mixture to boil.

Heat the brandy over medium heat in a separate small pan until it starts to fume. Do not heat too long or the alcohol content will burn off.

Pour the hot coffee mixture into a Brûlot Bowl. Put the Brûlot Bowl, the pan with the brandy, and a match on a flameproof serving platter. Bring the platter to the dinner table.

Turn down the dining room lights and then light the match. Hold the pan with the brandy over the Brûlot Bowl, and hold the match to the top of the pan with the brandy. The liquor will ignite. Extinguish the match and slowly pour the flaming brandy into the Brûlot Bowl. Do not let the alcohol flame for too long a time. Stir the coffee until the flames die.

Serve the hot coffee immediately in demitasse or regular coffee cups or, best of all, in Brûlot Cups. To keep the remaining coffee warm, soak the Brûlot Bowl burner with grain alcohol, ignite the burner, and put it under the bowl.

Yield: 8 servings.

There is a wonderful anecdote about Café Brûlot told by Esther Breckenridge. ''In the 1920s and 1930s, Cézar was a headwaiter at Arnaud's Restaurant in New Orleans. He was a Frenchman and had spent many years in the French Foreign Legion. He composed this song using a mixture of words from various languages he had heard. The tune has been likened to a theme from the first act of the opera *La Belle Hélène* by Jacques Offenbach. When customers at Arnaud's ordered Café Brûlot, he was called in to brew the beverage. His handsome face featured the type of eyebrows and mustache that gave him a diabolical look. The histrionic gestures he used while ladling the flaming Brûlot added to the ceremony, which everyone enjoyed, especially the out-of-towners.'' This is the song he sang; sorry there is no translation:

> EN REVENANT DU SANS VREE MON
> JUBILANT! JUBILANT!
> PAIN PAIN PI NA GO
> LA CABINETRE
> EN REVENANT DU SANS VREE MON
> ON ON ON ON ON!

Williana Pinkins is one of the finest cooks in New Orleans. Her magical culinary touch in preparing daily feasts has been enjoyed by the Dupuy family for over thirty years.

New Orleans Dinner Menus

For lagniappe, there are typical New Orleans Dinners listed below. However, in true Creole style the best combinations are discovered in your own wild imagination. When planning a meal, be sure to note the number of persons served by each recipe; if necessary, adjust the quantities of ingredients. If a particular appetizer or salad is not specified, you should select an appropriate one, or create one to complement the meal. Fresh French bread is a staple for most New Orleans meals.

HOLIDAY FEAST

ROAST TURKEY
CORN BREAD–OYSTER DRESSING
CHARLOTTE'S CRANBERRY SAUCE
BONNE MÈRE'S SWEET POTATO ORANGE CUPS
MUSHROOM RICE
ARTICHOKE CASSEROLE
MAMOU'S MOCHA ICE CREAM BOMBE
CAFÉ BRÛLOT DIABOLIQUE

GRAND-MÈRE'S DAUBE GLACÉ
RED BEANS AND RICE
BREADED PORK CHOPS
CARROT AND RAISIN SALAD
LILLY'S BISCUITS
BLACKBERRY PIE

AVOCADO DIP AND CRACKERS
GUMBO AND RICE
SALAD
FRENCH BREAD
VINSON'S PECAN PIE

OLIVE-CHEESE BALLS
GRILLADES AND GRITS
BAKED CUSHAW
LETTUCE FATIGUÉ
LEMON MERINGUE PIE

TOASTED PECANS
CRAWFISH BISQUE AND RICE
SALAD
FRENCH BREAD
MACAROON ICE CREAM DELIGHT

JALAPEÑO CORN BREAD
CRAWFISH ÉTOUFFÉE AND RICE
GRAPEFRUIT AND AVOCADO SALAD
FRENCH BREAD
CHEESECAKE WITH STRAWBERRY GLAZE

BARBECUED SHRIMP
TATEE'S OYSTER STEW
FRENCH BREAD
APPLE PIE

WILDER'S CHEESE BRIOCHE
SHRIMP CREOLE AND RICE
JERUSALEM ARTICHOKES WITH CREAM
  CHEESE SAUCE
FRENCH BREAD
CUP CUSTARD

CRAB QUICHE
VEGETABLE SOUP
COLESLAW
FRENCH BREAD
LEMON YUM-YUM CAKE

PÂTÉ IN CRUST
SOUP MEAT SALAD
FRENCH BREAD
PECAN BALLS

OYSTER AND MUSHROOM DIP
JAMBALAYA
EGG AND BACON SALAD
FRENCH BREAD
CHOCOLATE MOUSSE

CHIPPED BEEF DIP AND CRACKERS
CHICKEN FRICASSÉE AND RICE
SPINACH CASSEROLE
FRENCH BREAD
PEARS BELLE HÉLÈNE

OYSTERS ROCKEFELLER
PUDDIN'S SPAGHETTI SAUCE
FRENCH BREAD
CRÈME BRÛLÉE

GAZPACHO
EGGS SARDOU
FRENCH BREAD
MOCHA MOUSSE

FRIED OYSTERS WRAPPED IN BACON
ROAST LEG OF LAMB AND RICE
CREAMED SPINACH
FRENCH BREAD
BREAD PUDDING WITH WHISKEY SAUCE

RED BEAN DIP
BAKED MASHED SWEET POTATOES
BAKED HAM
SKILLET POLE BEANS
FRENCH BREAD
COCOA CAKE

CHEESE STRAWS
FRIED TROUT
CRAB MEAT AND ARTICHOKE CASSEROLE
FRENCH BREAD
ALEXIS' COCOONS AND FRESH FRUIT

DILL DIP AND CRACKERS
TROUT MARGUÉRY
SALAD
FRENCH BREAD
MAMA'S PRALINES

BAYOU PÂTÉ
FRIED CHICKEN
STUFFED MIRLITON
FRENCH BREAD
APPLE CREAM TART

CHEESE CROQUETTES
RICE AND ARTICHOKE HEARTS SALAD
FRENCH BREAD
CORN FLAKE ICE CREAM RING

APPETIZER
PÉPÈRE'S BEEF SCALLOPINI
PAPOU'S CHEESE SOUFFLÉ
CAESAR SALAD
FRENCH BREAD
ICE CREAM BALLS

SHRIMP RÉMOULADE
FRIED OYSTERS
STUFFED ARTICHOKE HEARTS
SALAD
MINTED WATERMELON

APPETIZER
CRAB MEAT AND GRAPEFRUIT SALAD
RED BEAN SOUP AND CROUTONS
PAPOU'S FIG PRESERVES, CHEESE AND
    CRACKERS

TROUT MOUSSE DIP
FRIED SOFT-SHELL CRABS WITH ALMONDS
FRENCH BREAD
SALAD
FLOATING ISLAND

TROUT PÂTÉ
AUNT LULU'S SHRIMP ÉTOUFFÉE
BREADSTICKS
SALAD
TANTE EMMA'S PEAR PRESERVES, CHEESE
    AND CRACKERS

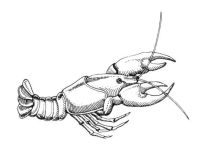

Glossary

AL DENTE (ahl den-TAY)—Is an Italian word meaning "to the tooth." It refers to the degree to which pasta is cooked. It is cooked to *al dente* when the texture gives a little resistance to the tooth. Pasta should be firm and have no raw flour taste. Cooking times will vary according to the thickness of the pasta.

BAYOU (BI-yoo)—A natural canal derived from the overflow of the river or marshes found in southern Louisiana and Mississippi. Cajuns live in the bayou country.

BISQUE (BISK)—A soup made with shellfish. When using crawfish, it is a rich thick soup with stuffed crawfish heads, served in a large bowl over rice.

BLEND—Blending or mixing is usually done by hand or with an electric blender or mixer. Food processors may be used at your own discretion.

BRIOCHE (BREE-osh)—A French word for a light bread rich with flour, butter, eggs, and yeast. However, in Cheese Brioche there is no yeast. Brioche can also mean "a blunder or mistake." For sweet brioche, see Pat's Mardi Gras King Cake (pages 128–30).

BRÛLOT BOWL (Brew-LOW)—See page 158. It is also great for serving hot dips. It is available at Loubat Restaurant Supplies, 510 Bienville Street, New Orleans, LA 70130, telephone 504-523-2811.

CAJUN (KAY-jun)—A French descendant from Acadia (Nova Scotia and New Brunswick), Canada, living in the Louisiana bayou countryside. *See* Creole.

CRAWFISH or Crayfish (pronounced in the south as KRAW-fish)—They are small (3 to 4 inches), freshwater crustaceans that resemble lobsters in shape. They are abundantly found in the bayou country. The local and national demand has grown so much that now there are many crawfish farms in Louisiana. Elsewhere, crawfish may possibly be found in specialty stores. If they are not available, for Étouffée, use large sea scallops instead of crawfish and delete crawfish fat. To eat crawfish: Remove the tail from the head. Pinch the tail shell until it cracks.

167

Turn the tail shell over so that the bottom-side is up. With both of your thumbs, push the shell toward the outside until it separates. Remove the tail meat. Use the meat as directed; remove the vein if desired. Much of the seasoned juice from cooking is in the head section of the crawfish. As they say in Louisiana, "Suck the head, it's delicious!"

CRAWFISH FAT—A yellowish-orange liquid found in the crawfish. However, it is best found in 1-ounce packages in Louisiana supermarkets.

CRAWFISH HEAD—Is the main body of the crawfish from which the claws, legs, and tail extend.

CRAWFISH TAIL—Is the end section of the crawfish in which the succulent tail meat is found.

CREAMS—A light cream is a table cream containing 18 percent to 30 percent milkfat. A heavy cream is a whipping cream containing 30 percent to 40 percent milkfat.

CREOLE (KREE-ole)—A French word meaning "native to the region, or born at home." Creole can be used to describe a variety of people in the Western Hemisphere. In Louisiana, it refers to the people of French and Spanish descent whose ancestors settled in New Orleans. Cajun refers to the environs south and southwest of New Orleans, and its people of French descent.

Through the centuries, "the city" and "the country" food styles have blended together so much that there is little distinction between the two. Many of the same dishes are served both in New Orleans homes and in country homes. If there are distinctions between Creole and Cajun, typical Creole recipes are Eggs Sardou, Grillades and Grits, Gumbo, Oysters Rockefeller, and Red Beans and Rice. A few typical Cajun recipes are Chicken Fricassée, Crawfish Bisque, Crawfish Étouffée, and Jambalaya.

ÉTOUFFÉE (ay-too FAY)—A French word for a stew. As a verb it means "to smother or braise." In cooking, it means "to smother or braise food in its own juices in a closed pot."

FILÉ (FEE-lay)—Is a powder derived from the sassafras leaf. It can be used for thickening and flavoring soups and gumbos. Filé is approved by the Food and Drug Administration. However, sassafras root is not approved.

FRICASSÉE (FRICK-a-see)—A French word meaning to sauté and then cook meat in its own gravy for a long time.

GARLIC CLOVES—The inner separate sections of the garlic bulb. Many Southern cooks refer to the garlic bulb as the garlic head, and the garlic clove as the garlic toe.

GRILLADES (gree-ODDS)—A French word meaning "grilled meat." In Creole cooking, it is thinly sliced top round beef, cooked slowly in a well-seasoned gravy.

GUMBO—The okra plant, or the edible, sticky pods of the plant. Also a thick soup made from okra or thickened with filé (ground sassafras leaves). The soup contains shrimp, crab, oyster, chicken, sausage, or other combinations, and is served in a large bowl over rice. It is also spelled Gombo and refers to a patois, or provincial dialect, spoken in New Orleans.

JAMBALAYA (jam-ba-LY-a)—A Creole dish made with rice and vegetables, and sausage, shrimp, pork, ham, chicken, turkey, or beef. The word jambalaya comes from the French word *jambon* for ham and the African word *ya* for rice. The *à la* means "with." Therefore, ham with rice.

JELLY ROLL PAN—A large flat baking sheet with sides (17¾ by 11¾ by ¾ inches).

KITCHEN BOUQUET—Is an all-natural liquid darkener for soups and gravies. It is made from caramel, salt, spices, water, celery, onions, carrots, parsnips, turnips, and parsley. If Kitchen Bouquet is not available, use a similar darkening liquid.

LAGNIAPPE (lan-YAP)—A small gift made to a customer, a little something extra, something for nothing.

MARGARINE—Can be used instead of butter because it has a lower cholesterol content.

MARINATE—To let vegetables, fish, or meat soak in a seasoned liquid for a period of time. The marinade is the liquid in which it soaks.

NEUTRAL GROUND—Is the section of land in the middle of the street known in most places as the median.

NEW ORLEANS (pronounced NAW-yuns, new-AW-yuns, or new-aw-LYUNS by locals)

OYSTER LIQUOR—The liquid in which shucked oysters are kept fresh in a container.

PARBOILED—To boil for a short time until partially cooked.

PASTRY BLENDER—A semicircle of five wires attached to a handle.

RING MOLD—A round mold shaped like a doughnut sliced in half horizontally (8½ by 2½ inches).

ROUX (ROO)—A French word meaning a "reddish-brown or rust color." In cooking, it is a mixture of oil and flour used for thickening sauces and soups. It is usually prepared in a heavy skillet until light or dark brown, depending on its use. If the roux burns, it should be discarded.

SAUTÉ—To quickly fry in a pan or skillet with a small amount of oil or butter until the ingredient is light brown.

SCALD—To heat a liquid until it begins to vaporize and before it boils.

SCALLION—A long thin green onion.

SEAR—To cook meat quickly in order to lock in the juices.

SHALLOT—A small onion shaped like garlic.

SOUPÇON (soup-SAHN)—A French word meaning suspicion or conjecture. A tiny pinch of an ingredient.

STEAM—To cook ingredients in a steamer basket to retain their maximum nutritional value. If a steamer basket is not available, use a colander over a pot of boiling water.

TABASCO—A trademarked name for the condiment of red pepper, vinegar, and salt made on Avery Island in New Iberia, Louisiana.

TO TASTE—Many Creole recipes call for amounts of spicy ingredients which may be too hot for some people and not hot enough for others. When using salt, black pepper, or cayenne pepper why not cook New Orleans style . . . "to taste."

TO TURN—To separate or curdle.

UNBLEACHED WHITE FLOUR—Is used instead of bleached white flour because it contains fewer chemicals.

Mail-Order Information for Louisiana Products

Creole Delicacies Company
533 Saint Ann Street
New Orleans, LA 70116
504-525-9508
> Attn: Mail Order Department
> Items available: Southern Pecans, Louisiana Navel Oranges, Beignet Mix, Coffee and Chicory, Pralines, New Orleans soups (Shrimp Creole, Gumbo, Turtle, Crawfish Bisque), Rémoulade Sauce, Hot Pepper Jelly, Praline Sauce, Cane Syrup, Red Beans and Rice, and Famous Drinks of New Orleans Recipe Book

Zatarain's Inc.
82 First Street
P.O. Box 347
Gretna, LA 70053
504-367-2950
> Attn: Mail Order Department
> Items available: special New Orleans seasonings—Seasoned Fish Fri, Fish Fri, Crab Boil, Liquid Crab Boil, Creole Mustard, and Gumbo Filé

Evans Creole Candy Co., Inc.
848 Decatur Street
New Orleans, LA 70116
504-522-7111
> Attn: Mail Order Department
> Items available: Creole Chocolate Fudge, Pecan Slices, Old-Fashioned Coconut Kraut, Pecan Log, Praline Syrup, Cuccia Chocolates, Turtles (chocolate-caramel and pecans), Creole Hash (chocolate-pecans clustered in marshmallow), Chocolate Covered Cherries, Evans Creole Candy Cookbook, Chewie Pralines, and Pralines (Pecan, Chocolate, Rum, and Maple)

Louisiana Seafood
4418 Downman Road
New Orleans, LA 70126
504-245-1661
  Attn: Mail Order Department
  Items available: Fresh Shrimp, Red Fish, Catfish, Sheepshead, Boiled Crabs, Lump Crab Meat, Oysters, Crawfish, and other seafood available when in season

Many thanks to:

Jerry Allen
Randy Allen
Ray Allen
Sue Allen
Vince Allen
Billie Begue
Mary Begue
Esther Breckenridge
Kitty Brewer
Lillian Brown
Peggy Brown
Linda Jeanne Brownell
Alice Marie Buckalew
Jacquie Calnan
Anne Ching
Carol Ching
Michael Del Colliano
Pat Couret
Madame Courteaud
Betty Cutler
Lucinda Denton
Barbara Dohman
Charlotte Dupuy
Homer Dupuy
Peter Dupuy
Seph Dupuy
Haydée Ellis
Steve Ellis
Aunt Emma
Michele Galatoire
Diana Gonzalez
Grand-Mère
Grand-Père
Judith Grezaffi
Betsy Hartson
Liza Hartson
Lottie Hillyer
Mary Hillyer
Pappy Hillyer
Historic New
  Orleans Collection

Hal Hoiland
Louise Jastram
Linda Jemison
Leigh Jennings
Nana Kappes
Poppy Kappes
Paris Keena
Don Kroll
Stephanie Lamar
Aunt Leah
The Library of Congress
Aunt Lulu
Clare McGowan
Lynn McManus
Caroline Macon
Ellen Masin-Persina
Amy Matthews
Bill Matthews
Sandy Matthews
Ineke Meuter
The National Archives
Alexis Navarro
Suzanne Nolan
Williana Pinkins
Kathy Plunket
Jackson Polk
Alberte Pullman
Bernard Pullman
Erika Rainone
Iris Rainone
Jan Reber
Louise Reed
Dorothee Riederer
Bridget Robey
Raymond St. Pierre
Wilder Selman
Marie Sharp
Emily Sheketoff
Lynne Sims-Taylor
Rolande Soulier
Judy Stoewe

Tante Mae
Ann Taylor
Sylvianne Tramier
Tim Trapolin
Kathleen Vadnal
Suzanne Vizard

Katie Walshe
Betty Wason
Vicky Westover
Doug White
Wendy White
Marilyn Williams

Index

Alexis' Cocoons, 136
Almonds
  fried soft-shell crabs with, 67
  mocha ice cream bombe, Mamou's, 152
Appetizers
  Avocado Dip, 2
  cheese brioche, Wilder's, 8
  Cheese Straws, 7
  Chipped Beef Dip, 4
  Crab Quiche, 17
  daube glacé, Grand-Mère's, 13–14
  Dill Dip, 3
  Olive-Cheese Balls, 6
  Oyster and Mushroom Dip, 5
  Oysters Rockefeller, 16–17
  oysters wrapped in bacon, fried, 15
  pâté, bayou, 12
  Pâté in Crust, 10–11
  pecans, toasted, 20
  Red Bean Dip, 2
  shrimp, barbecued, 19
  Shrimp Rémoulade, 18–19
  Trout Mousse Dip, 4–5
  Trout Pâté, 9–10
Apple
  cream tart, 142–143
  pie, 138
Artichoke(s)
  casserole, 83
  casserole, crab meat and, 68
  casserole, oyster and, 83

hearts, salad of rice and, 102
hearts, stuffed, 84
steamed, 82
see also Jerusalem artichokes
Aunt Lulu's Shrimp Étouffée, 29
Avocado
  dip, 2
  salad, grapefruit and, 103

Bacon
  and egg salad, 103
  oysters wrapped in fried, 15
Balls
  cheese, fried (croquettes), 37
  ice cream, 151
  olive-cheese, 6
  pecan, 137
Bananas, fried, 86
Barbecue
  chicken, 54–55
  ribs, 51
  shrimp, 19
Bayou Pâté, 12
Béarnaise Sauce, 108–109
Béchamel Sauce, 110
Beef
  dip, chipped, 4
  Grillades and Grits, 44
  Jambalaya, 78
  Meat Loaf, 48
  po-boy, hot roast, 39
  pot roast, Williana's, 45

ribs, barbecued, 51
scallopini, Pépère's,
42–43
Soup Meat Salad, 100
spaghetti sauce, Puddin's,
46–47
Biscuits, Lilly's, 124
Bisque, crawfish, 25–26
Blackberry Pie, 139
Bombe, mocha ice cream,
Mamou's, 152
Bonne Mère's Sweet Potato
Orange Cups, 92
Bread
biscuits, Lilly's, 124
cinnamon, pull-apart, 118–
119
Corn Bread-Oyster
Dressing, 114–115
Croutons, 125
crumbs, 15
jalapeño corn, 120–121
lost (*Pain Perdu*), 123
pudding with whiskey
sauce, 148–149
-sticks, 124–125
whole wheat-honey, 122
Breadsticks, 124–125
Brioche, cheese, Wilder's, 8

Caesar Salad, 101
Café Brûlot Diabolique, 158–
159
Cake
Cheesecake with
Strawberry Glaze, 134–
135
cocoa, 131

king, Pat's Mardi Gras, 128–
130
lemon yum-yum, 132–133
Candy
date nut roll, Gran's, 157
pralines, Mama's, 156
Carrot and Raisin Salad, 105
Casserole
artichoke, 83
artichoke-oyster, 83
crabmeat and artichoke, 68
spinach, 95
Charlotte's Cranberry Sauce,
113
Cheese
brioche, Wilder's, 8
-cake with strawberry glaze,
134–135
croquettes (Fried Cheese
Balls), 37
Jalapeño Corn Bread, 120–
121
Jerusalem Artichokes with
Cream Cheese Sauce, 85
macaroni and, baked, 75
Olive-Cheese Balls, 6
sauce, 110
soufflé, Papou's, 36
straws, 7
Cheesecake with Strawberry
Glaze, 134–135
Chicken
barbecued, 54
fricassée, 56
fried, 55
Jambalaya, 78
and sausage gumbo, 27
Véronique, 57
Chipped Beef Dip, 4

Chocolate
  Cocoa Cake, 131
  Mocha Mousse, 149
  mousse, 150
  sauce, for Pears Belle
    Hélène, 155
Choron Sauce, 109
Cinnamon bread, pull-apart,
  118–119
Cocoa Cake, 131
Cocoons, Alexis', 136
Coffee
  Café Brûlot Diabolique, 158–
    159
  Mocha Mousse, 149
Coleslaw, 104–105
Cookies
  cocoons, Alexis', 136
  Pecan Balls, 137
Corn bread, jalapeño, 120–121
Corn Bread-Oyster Dressing,
  114–115
Corn Flake Ice Cream Ring,
  153
Corn Pudding Soufflé, 35
Courtbouillon, red fish, 64
Crab/crabmeat
  with almonds, fried soft-
    shell, 67
  and artichoke casserole, 68
  and grapefruit salad, 100–101
  quiche, 17
  rémoulade, 19
  Seafood Gumbo, 27
Cranberry sauce, Charlotte's,
  113
Crawfish
  bisque, 25–26
  étouffée, 30

Creamed Tuna on Toast, 71
Crème Brûlée, 144–145
Croquettes, cheese (Fried
  Cheese Balls), 37
Croutons, 125
Cup Custard, 145
Cushaw, baked, 96
Custard
  Crème Brûlée, 144–145
  cup, 145
  Floating Island, 146–147

Date nut roll, Gran's, 157
Daube glacé, Grand-Mère's,
  13–14
Dill Dip, 3
Dip
  avocado, 2
  chipped beef, 4
  dill, 3
  oyster and mushroom, 5
  red bean, 2
  trout mousse, 4–5
Dressing
  corn bread-oyster, 114–115
  Vinaigrette, 112
  vinegar and oil, 112
  see also Sauce

Eggs
  and bacon salad, 103
  sardou, 34–35
Étouffée
  crawfish, 30
  shrimp, Aunt Lulu's, 29

Fig preserves, Papou's, 115
Floating Island, 146–147
French Toast, 123

Fricassée, chicken, 56
Frosting, for Cocoa Cake, 131

Gazpacho, 22
Glaze, strawberry, for
    cheesecake, 134–135
Grand-Mère's Daube Glacé,
    13–14
Grand-Mère's Roasted Quail,
    59–61
Gran's Date Nut Roll, 157
Grapefruit
    and avocado salad, 103
    salad, crab meat and, 100–
        101
Gravy
    for roast beef, 42
    for roast turkey, 58
Grillades and Grits, 44
Grits
    baked, 79
    boiled, 79
    grillades and, 44
Gumbo
    chicken and sausage, 27
    seafood, 27
    turkey, 28

Ham
    baked, 48–49
    Jambalaya, 78
Hollandaise Sauce, 108
Honey, whole wheat bread
    with, 122

Ice Cream
    balls, 151
    macaroon delight, 154

mocha bombe, Mamou's,
    152
ring, corn flake, 153

Jalapeño Corn Bread, 120–121
Jambalaya, 78
Jerusalem artichokes
    with cream cheese sauce, 85
    steamed, 84–85

King cake, Pat's Mardi Gras,
    128–130

Lamb leg, roast, 52
Lemon
    meringue pie, 140
    yum-yum cake, 132–133
Lettuce Fatigué, 106
Lilly's Biscuits, 124
Lost Bread, 123

Macaroni and cheese, baked,
    75
Macaroons
    ice cream delight, 154
    mocha ice cream bombe,
        Mamou's, 152
Mama's Pralines, 156
Mamou's Mocha Ice Cream
    Bombe, 152
Mardi Gras king cake, Pat's,
    128–130
Mayonnaise, 111
Meat Loaf, 48
Minted Watermelon, 154
Mirliton
    baked, 97
    stuffed, 98

Mocha
  ice cream bombe,
    Mamou's, 152
  mousse, 149
Mousse
  chocolate, 150
  dip, trout, 4–5
  mocha, 149
Mushroom
  dip, oyster and, 5
  rice, 77

Nut roll, Gran's date and, 157

Olive-Cheese Balls, 6
Orange cup, sweet potato,
    Bonne Mère's, 92
Oysters
  Artichoke-Oyster
    Casserole, 83
  Corn Bread-Oyster
    Dressing, 114–115
  fried, 69
  and mushroom dip, 5
  po-boy, fried, 38–39
  Rockefeller, 16–17
  stew, Tatee's, 31
  wrapped in bacon, fried, 15

Pain Perdu, 123
Papou's Cheese Soufflé, 36
Papou's Fig Preserves, 115
Pasta
  macaroni and cheese,
    baked, 75
  manicotti, stuffed, 74–75
  spaghetti sauce, Puddin's,
    46–47

Pastry
  Pâté in Crust, 10–11
  plain, 143
Pâté
  bayou, 12
  in crust, 10–11
  trout, 9–10
Pat's Mardi Gras King Cake,
    128–130
Pears
  belle Hélène, 155
  preserves, Tante Emma's,
    116
Pecans
  balls, 137
  date nut roll, Gran's, 157
  pie, Vinson's, 141
  pralines, Mama's, 156
  toasted, 20
Pépère's Beef Scallopini, 42–
    43
Pie
  apple, 138
  blackberry, 139
  lemon meringue, 140
  pecan, Vinson's, 141
  raspberry, 139
Po-boys
  oyster, fried, 38–39
  roast beef, hot, 39
  shrimp, fried, 39
Pole beans, skillet, 87
Pork
  chops, breaded, 49
  chops, glazed, 50
  Jambalaya, 78
  ribs, barbecued, 51
  spaghetti sauce, Puddin's,
    46–47

Potato(es)
  mashed, 90
  puffs, 91
  salad, 104
Pot roast, Williana's, 45
Pralines, Mama's, 156
Preserves
  fig, Papou's, 115
  pear, Tante Emma's, 116
Pudding
  bread, with whiskey sauce,
    148–149
  corn soufflé, 35
Puddin's Spaghetti Sauce, 46–
  47
Pull-Apart Cinnamon Bread,
  118–119

Quail, roasted, Grand-Mère's,
  59–61
Quiche, crab, 17

Raisin salad, carrot and, 105
Raspberry Pie, 139
Red Beans
  dip, 2
  and rice, 88–89
  soup, 24
Red Fish Courtbouillon, 64
Ribs, barbecued, 51
Rice
  and artichoke hearts salad,
    102
  mushroom, 77
  red beans and, 88–89
  steamed, 76

Salad
  Caesar, 101
  carrot and raisin, 105

Coleslaw, 104–105
crab meat and grapefruit,
  100–101
egg and bacon, 103
grapefruit and avocado, 103
Lettuce Fatigué, 106
potato, 104
rice and artichoke hearts,
  102
soup meat, 100
Sandwiches
  oyster, fried, 38–39
  roast beef, hot, 39
  shrimp, fried, 39
Sauce
  barbecue, for ribs, 51
  béarnaise, 108–109
  béchamel, 110
  cheese, 110
  chocolate, for Pears Belle
    Hélène, 155
  choron, 109
  cranberry, Charlotte's, 113
  cream cheese, for Jerusalem
    artichokes, 85
  hollandaise, 108
  Mayonnaise, 111
  rémoulade, for shrimp, 18
  spaghetti, Puddin's 46–47
  tartare, 111
  tomato, for stuffed
    manicotti, 74
  whiskey, for bread pudding,
    148–149
Sausage
  and chicken gumbo, 27
  Jambalaya, 78
Scallopini, Pépère's beef, 42–
  43

Seafood Gumbo, 27
Shrimp
  barbecued, 19
  Creole, 70
  étouffée, Aunt Lulu's, 29
  fried, 69
  Jambalaya, 78
  po-boy, fried, 39
  rémoulade, 18–19
  Seafood Gumbo, 27
Skillet Pole Beans, 87
Soft-shell crabs with almonds,
  fried, 67
Soufflé
  cheese, Papou's, 36
  corn pudding, 35
Soup
  Crawfish Bisque, 25–26
  Crawfish Étouffée, 30
  Gazpacho, 22
  red bean, 24
  Red Fish Courtbouillon,
    64
  Seafood Gumbo, 27
  shrimp étouffée, Aunt
    Lulu's, 29
  Turkey Gumbo, 28
  vegetable, 22–23
Spinach
  casserole, 95
  creamed, 94
Squash
  cushaw, baked, 96
  mirliton, baked, 97
  mirliton, stuffed, 98
Stew, oyster, Tatee's, 31
Strawberries
  Corn Flake Ice Cream Ring,
    153

glaze, for cheesecake, 134–
  135
Sweet Potatoes
  baked mashed, 93
  orange cups, Bonne Mère's,
    92

Tante Emma's Pear
  Preserves, 116
Tart, apple cream, 142–143
Tartare Sauce, 111
Tatee's Oyster Stew, 31
Tomato sauce, for Stuffed
  Manicotti, 74
Topping for Lemon Yum-
  Yum Cake, 132–133
Trout
  fried, 65
  Marguéry, 66
  mousse dip, 4–5
  pâté, 9–10
Tuna on toast, creamed, 71
Turkey
  with gravy, roast, 58
  gumbo, 28
  Jambalaya, 78

Veal
  chops, breaded, 49
  scallopini, 43
Vegetables
  Artichoke Casserole, 83
  artichoke hearts, stuffed, 84
  artichokes, steamed, 82
  bananas, fried, 86
  cushaw, baked, 96
  Jerusalem artichokes,
    steamed, 84–85

Jerusalem Artichokes with
  Cream Cheese Sauce, 85
mirliton, baked, 97
mirliton, stuffed, 98
pole beans, skillet, 87
potatoes, mashed, 90
Potato Puffs, 91
Potato Salad, 104
Red Beans and Rice, 88–89
soup, 22–23
spinach, creamed, 94
Spinach Casserole, 95
sweet potatoes, baked
  mashed, 93

sweet potato orange cups,
  Bonne Mère's, 92
Vinaigrette, 112
Vinegar and Oil Dressing, 112
Vinson's Pecan Pie, 141

Watermelon, minted, 154
Whiskey sauce, bread pudding
  with, 148–149
Whole Wheat-Honey Bread,
  122
Wilder's Cheese Brioche, 8
Williana's Pot Roast, 45

MA!